WESTERN EUROPEAN LANGUAGES

A Reference Guide

Ian James Parsley

Independently published by *Ultonia Publishing* **(Belfast)**

Distributed by *Ultonia Language Services*

ISBN   9-7986934565-2-5

5   20

UK £9.95   US $11.95

ACKNOWLEDGEMENTS

——

I am greatly indebted to those who have inspired, encouraged and assisted me in my linguistic journey, and particularly in my objective of bringing a range of languages to a wider audience.

Thanks are due to Alex Godwin, based in Hamburg, a friend for longer than either of us cares to remember, who was an essential support for German and Italian. Regarding the modern Romance languages in general, another longstanding friend Marc Leprêtre, based in Barcelona, was a huge and always cheerful assistance. It is safe to say that there would be no chapter on Afrikaans without my own cousin, Byron Forbes, and his wife Bianca, based in the Cape. Here in Northern Ireland I was also fortunate to have Pedro Delgado, a native of Venezuela, to provide advice on Spanish in its various forms; Anna Murray, who grew up in Jutland, to help with Danish; as well as Claudia Valerio and Paul Sinclair, who kindly offered their experience specifically with the different varieties of Portuguese.

Last but far from least is of course my wife Paula, whose patience is ever tested but whose love remains ever present.

Ian James Parsley, Belfast, October 2020

PREFACE

This handbook is designed to be a simple reference guide for people wishing to use or learn the major languages of Western Europe, which are particularly notable for how they have spread across the world.

It is written to serve a purpose for people regardless of their language learning goals, ranging from those who wish to use languages for professional reasons through to those for whom they are simply a hobby. The aim is to provide a platform for deeper study of any individual language or group of languages as appropriate. It can be used by people entirely new to languages as a foundation, by people who already speak one language to learn a related one, or by people who just want a reference for broadening linguistic study. It is set out so that each chapter can stand alone; the user can choose whether to read the entire book from front to back, or to keep it for occasional reference.

This book is not intended as a linguistic textbook. A balance was sought to ensure the user is not overburdened with linguistic terminology, but also that explanation is clear and concise. Where technical terms are necessarily used, these are explained immediately in the text where possible; however, for further assistance, a glossary of terms is appended.

Why is the focus only on languages which developed initially in Western Europe? Ultimately, it is these languages which have spread out to the Americas, Australasia and elsewhere to become official or national in most countries across the globe. As a result, anyone familiar with the major Latinate/Romance and Germanic languages will be able to travel and be understood not just across Western Europe, but across much of the world.

Historical languages were a late inclusion to this handbook, as it became clear that some focus on them would serve to enhance understanding of the heritage of Western European languages and how they are interconnected. It is hoped that this will provide further interest, as well as a firmer grounding for learners to recognize connections even between modern languages.

> Throughout the book, analysis is added in grey boxes consisting either of technical grammatical information or sociolinguistic commentary. This can be ignored when focusing on the main text; it is included merely for further detail or general interest.

Language learning is at a crossroads. The way in which languages are taught in schools, particularly in the English-speaking world, has not caught up with developments in both technology and linguistics over recent years. Too many pupils leave school believing themselves "not good at languages". This is a serious problem, because with the right strategy language learning can be both accessible and fun for everyone.

This book aims to complement the significant advances and broader debates around language learning which have been made in the Internet age. In that context, it is inevitable that contributions such as this will themselves be subject to debate. This is a good thing, as it demonstrates people are passionate about languages and about the ways in which they can be used and promoted more effectively. For as long as that debate is well informed, it can only enhance language learning. If this book encourages more of that informed debate, it will have achieved a further purpose.

Although many individuals have offered great expertise to me during the development of this work and it has been meticulously researched and checked, it is almost inevitable when covering so many languages that there will be errors or omissions. I alone am responsible for these.

Ian James Parsley, Belfast, October 2020

CONTENTS

CONTENTS

INTRODUCTION

The aim of this handbook is to provide a basic grounding in each major national language of Western Europe, thereby covering all Latinate (also known as Italic or Romance) and Germanic languages with over 25 million mother tongue speakers, and a set of languages spoken natively by over a quarter of the global population. By coming to recognize the basics of each, and understanding something of the links between them, we can develop a platform to become proficient in new languages swiftly and thus communicate with billions of people world-wide.

It is worth emphasizing also that proficiency in a foreign language does not mean knowing everything; it means having sufficient knowledge to develop understanding in the language without recourse to English.

0.1   Phonology

To be proficient in any language, of course we need to know how it is pronounced. At the start, the basics are sufficient – most individual consonants are pronounced similarly in any language, so the main challenges are with the vowels, the diphthongs (two vowels pronounced together), and perhaps some awkward consonant clusters (consonants appearing directly after each other).

Over time, it pays to mimic the rhythm and intonation of the target language. To speak Italian like a Cockney or French with a Texan accent is like trying to learn the words of a song without the tune. We will never get it absolutely perfect, but we do want to get to the stage where we are not immediately identifiable as an English speaker, not least because being identified as an English speaker makes it harder to practise if the other person knows (or thinks they know) English.

A key phonological point for beginners is that not all letters are entirely individual. Many are in fact closely related to each other, and this can have an impact on how they change from language to language. For example, pairs such as /b/ and /p/, /v/ and /f/, /g/ and /k/ or /z/ and /s/ are in each case voiced and voiceless versions of what is otherwise the same sound; some languages may distinguish these or prefer one over another (and others may not).

Hugely significant also are the location of articulation (some languages are simply pronounced farther forward or back, or up or down, in the mouth) and how stress works (most though not all languages stress one particular syllable in the word, but exactly how they do so varies; some also have long and short vowels and these may or may not be connected to stress).

0.2   Standard

When we learn a language, we in fact specifically learn the standard version of that language. Each modern Western European national language has a written standard form; knowing something about how this has developed is useful to understanding the interconnection between written and spoken versions of a single language, as well as between standard forms of different languages.

These standards have developed in different ways – some gradually through time via constant updating, some based on intentionally conservative usage of a dialect associated with a particular group of people or a geographical area, and some as deliberate mergers of dialects. Exactly how deliberately standards were developed and how readily they are accepted by speakers varies from case to case. Learners will also wish to determine from the outset whether they wish to focus on the spoken or the written language.

0.3   Vocabulary

Vocabulary is the priority for learning a language – without it, progress will always be extremely limited. There are three key aspects to it at the outset.

Firstly, it is useful to have a basic idea of where most of the vocabulary in any language comes from. This is often quite easy – most Italian words come from Latin. However, it can be tricky – English itself is a Germanic language, yet much of its vocabulary is directly or indirectly from Latin. Knowing this means we can take a reasonable guess at understanding even vocabulary we have never specifically learned (often, the key to proficiency is to get around what we do not know).

Secondly, we will want a reasonable list of pronouns/determiners (including articles) and common prepositions – in English, such words include 'me', 'that', 'the' and 'to'. These do not translate directly from language to language (indeed, very few items of vocabulary do), but it is necessary at least to recognize most of them at the outset, and then to begin to use them by mimicking the patterns we hear (or read).

Thirdly, we want to know the broader core vocabulary – words which are used regularly are essential to expressing and understanding things. Again, the key is to work around what we do not know; for example, although ideally we will recognize it when we hear it, we do not absolutely need to know the word for 'often', provided we can say 'nearly always' or 'sometimes'.

0.4   Grammar

Grammar is often a dreaded aspect of language learning because it is often taught in unnecessary detail at the outset. The good news is that a vast knowledge of grammar is not necessary to making considerable progress in most languages. The only requirement at the start is to have an outline, and to know some of the quirks to look out for. The detail will come freely and naturally once we start using the language regularly.

Firstly, we want to know the basics about how nouns work – they or the words around them may or may not be marked for number (in English, singular or plural), gender (masculine, feminine, neuter) or case (in English, direct 'they' versus oblique 'them'; many languages have far more cases than this and expand them beyond pronouns).

Secondly, we will want to know how verbs work – they may or may not be marked for tense (in English, past or present), aspect (whether ongoing and/or relevant, e.g. 'I have been', 'I am being') or to "agree" with the subject ('I like', 'she like<u>s</u>'). The verb or verb phrase may also be marked for mood (indicative, imperative or subjunctive) or voice (in English, active 'I like' or passive 'I am liked').

It is worth noting that tense is a peculiarly Indo-European thing; languages around the world often have verbal systems which prioritize the evidential basis of the action (whether the speaker felt it; saw it; heard about it first-hand; heard about it from other sources; etc), and some have no concept of time within their structure or vocabulary whatsoever. The comparative obsession with tense is itself a relatively recent innovation within Indo-European – thousands of years ago, the focus was more on mood and aspect (essentially on relevance to the current situation rather than on a specific point in time).

Thirdly, we may want to know how adjectives work – they may or may not agree with nouns; they may behave differently in different contexts; and they may or may not take the same form as adverbs.

Fourthly, we will want to know at least the fundamentals of how clauses are structured, including the main word order (English is generally "subject, verb, object" or "SVO"; some languages use varying word order depending on context), negation, and connecting words ('He came <u>but</u> you stayed', 'I saw <u>that</u> she was here', etc).

There are also particles (words used to express grammatical relationship with no specific meaning of their own), as well as how to express questions or exclamations, and so on.

This seems a lot for a basic grounding, but it can be done in stages – as we become exposed to a language we will soon work out how nouns work, then verbs (and put those together), then adjectives (add those to the mix), then structure, picking up particles as we go along.

0.5   Character

What is character? Knowing a language's character is as relevant as anything to making progress towards proficiency.

Firstly, we want to know the background to the language. Where does it come from? What influences are contained within it? For example, English is a Germanic language heavily influenced by Norman French, marked also by a significant sound shift from around 1350 to 1600. Knowing this means we can make sense of why the vocabulary is the way it is (with basic words generally of Germanic origin, but high culture words often similar to French or Latin), why the spelling appears so odd, and even to some extent why the grammatical structure is comparatively simple.

Secondly, we may want to know whether the language tends towards being predominantly noun-focused or verb-focused – in other words, does it build clauses predominantly around nouns (objects and facts) or verbs (actions)? This is general (no language is absolutely one way or the other) but having some idea of this provides a real feeling right at the outset for how the language is used.

Thirdly, languages do not stand alone – they are products of culture, at least to some extent. While nobody gains from lazy stereotypes, we can gain from knowing something of the character and culture of those who use any given language in order to use it ourselves.

1

INDO-EUROPEAN

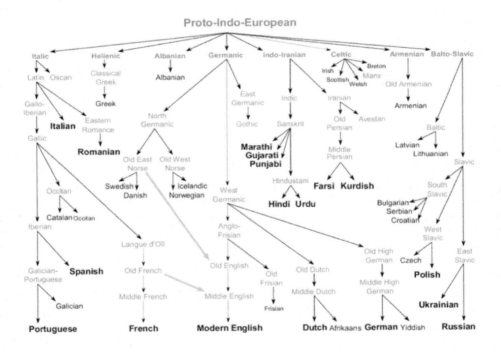

The "family tree" of Indo-European languages provides a slightly simplistic but nevertheless useful overview of how most of the languages spoken across Europe (and ultimately the Americas and Australasia), parts of the Middle East and much of the northern Indian subcontinent have developed.

We can see from it that a wide range of languages, including all the national languages of Europe bar Finnish, Estonian, Hungarian and Maltese, are derived from a single tongue likely spoken until around 4500 years ago, probably in or near modern Ukraine, which we now call Proto-Indo-European (PIE). Almost half the world's population speak a daughter language of PIE natively, and a majority live in countries whose prime administrative languages are descended from it.

As people moved about and conditions changed, PIE itself broke up over the centuries into different dialects which exhibited language change as they encountered new things to describe and came into contact with other languages.

For this reason, it is a good idea for any linguistic journey to begin with PIE itself.

1.1   Phonology

Clearly, we do not know at the distance of nearly five millennia exactly what PIE sounded like. However, through reconstruction, we can work out that it had the distinction versus modern languages of containing a lot of various sounds similar to those typically represented by modern English <h> and <l>. Most of these have been lost, but we can tell they existed from the way words and sounds developed subsequently.

We can reliably guess more about consonants than about vowels, although we do know that the most commonly occurring vowels were /e/ and /o/ (or close to them). Among consonants, there was a distinction between voiced (e.g. /b/), voiceless (e.g. /p/) and aspirated (similar to Classical Latin <ph>; although recent studies suggest that all aspirated consonants were voiced in PIE). There would also have been considerably more individual consonant sounds than in most modern Western European languages.

Most noteworthy of all, perhaps, is the evidence from daughter languages that PIE relied on pitch rather than stress; and that this was applied at the start of words (with the possible exception of words with prefixes). This would have given it a markedly different sound and rhythm from any modern Western European language.

1.2   Standard

Proto-Indo-European speakers had not, of course, developed the technology of writing. Written forms of the language are, therefore, necessarily the reconstructions of academic linguists using modern alphabets.

1.3   Vocabulary

Most of our vocabulary originates from PIE (although in fact this share is generally lower for Germanic languages such as English than it is for languages derived from Latin).

Key numbers:
1 hoi-no-, 2 dwo-, 3 trei, 4 kwetwor-, 5 penkwe, 6 sweks, 7 septm, 8 oktou; 9 newn 'nine, new number'; *10 dekm* 'ten'; *k'm.tóm* 'a large number'.

There is some evidence that counting may initially have been octal (base eight) rather than decimal (base ten). The word for 'hundred' in daughter languages is derived from *k'm.tóm*.

PIE did have identifiable nouns, verbs and adjectives (this is not the case for all languages world-wide). However, other word classes were less discernible – what are now prepositions, for example, were often postpositions or grammatical affixes.

1.4   Grammar

Nouns in PIE had eight, perhaps nine, cases – that is, nouns were marked by endings to distinguish whether they were being used as a subject, a direct object, an indirect object, a possessor, a recipient, and so on. They were also marked for three numbers (singular, dual and plural) and three genders (masculine, feminine, neuter), and often fell into a number of other classifications; for example, some were marked with the ending -r to show family relationship (a feature still current in almost all daughter languages, cf. English 'mother', 'brother', 'sister', etc).

Verbs were also marked, either by changes to the root vowel or by an ending (or both), primarily for aspect (not specifically tense, as such, but rather extension through time and how relevant the action is to the current time). There were also complex moods, essentially marking whether the action was certain, optional, counter-factual, and so on. Verbs could also be marked directly for the passive (effectively switching the subject and object around) or reflexive (making the subject also the object). They came in four classes, marked by the stem vowels (i.e. the vowel appearing last before the ending) /a/, /e/, /i/ or none. They were further classified inherently by aspect – as expressing a state, reflecting a state, reflecting incomplete action, reflecting ongoing action, or reflecting causative action (thus, where in English it is correct to say both 'he boils the water' and 'the water boils', PIE would not have allowed the same form of the verb for each).

Common (thematic) verb endings (1st, 2nd and 3rd person):
- Singular: -oh, -esi, -eti;
- Plural: -omos, -ete, -onti.

Dual endings also existed, but they are harder to reconstruct accurately (and are in any case not relevant to modern Western European languages).

All adjectives agreed with nouns; it is unclear how much distinction there was between adjectives and adverbs.

Pronouns were markedly different from how we currently understand them. There were first and second person pronouns (as modern English 'I', 'you', 'us', etc) but not third person (so no 'he', 'her', 'it', 'they').

Personal pronouns:

	Singular (1st, 2nd person)		Plural (1st, 2nd person)	
Nominative	*h,eg'oH*	*tuH*	*wei*	*yuH*
Accusative	*h,me'*	*twe'*	*nsme'*	*usme'*

Word order was generally SOV (subject, object, verb), although a range of cases (and other marker particles) would have allowed significant variation for emphasis and there was a shift in some dialects late on to SVO. The key negative particle was *ne*, although it is likely that there were many ways of negating clauses.

1.5   Character

Clearly, it is hard to assess the character of a language spoken thousands of years ago by such unfamiliar people in such an unfamiliar environment. We do not know exactly what its own origins were, or whether they were shared with any other currently existing language tree (this is still keenly debated by academics, but it seems unlikely).

Nevertheless, we do know something about the culture of PIE speakers. The structure of the language tells us that their society was clearly based around family units, and that it was somewhat patriarchal. There is evidence that PIE speakers were more accomplished with horses than other contemporary groups, which in large part explains why they were able to spread so comparatively quickly and why their language in its various dialects came to be spoken over such a large area. Much of this too, however, remains keenly debated and is constantly further informed by breakthroughs in both linguistics and archaeology.

2

CLASSICAL LATIN

Classical Latin, by which we generally mean the Golden Age Latin of Cicero (i.e. that spoken and written by the educated classes in Rome from just over 2000 years ago), is the version whose grammatical and broad orthographical norms are still what is understood by "Latin" when it is taught. This was the direct descendant of Early Latin (spoken from around 2700 years ago) and ancestor of Late Latin (discussed in Chapter 3). Furthermore, Classical Latin remained a single written *lingua franca* throughout the medieval era, particularly in ecclesiastical, philosophical and scientific life, and is still widely known and learned (and even in some cases, typically at specific conferences, spoken) in its Golden Age form.

Early Latin was initially spoken by a small tribe based in and slightly to the south (i.e. within easy modern commuting distance) of Rome, in the region which eventually became known as Latium (modern Italian *Lazio*); to the north was spoken the closely related Faliscan, and around it were other Italic languages alongside some tongues of non-Indo-European origin and Ionian Greek (spoken along the coast well to the south). Latin spread across the Italian peninsula, largely displacing all other languages by the Golden Age period and completely displacing them by around AD 100 (another Italic language, Oscan, is particularly well attested because it was still in use alongside Latin in Pompeii at the time of its destruction, but it seems to have gone extinct within a generation after that). From before the time of Christ *sermō vulgāris,* which can be literally translated as "popular speech" but is more commonly known as "Vulgar Latin", was brought to all corners of the

Empire by legionaries and other administrators. After the conquest of any individual province by the Romans, Latin was not formally enforced on the local population but in practice either it or Greek were required for trade and administration, and for that reason within a few generations typically Latin had taken over in common use.

2.1   Phonology

The phonology of Classical Latin has been subject to much debate. In time it gave way to daughter languages, sometimes sharing phonological developments with each other and sometimes displaying their own. Speakers of those languages, and even of English and German, came to pronounce Latin (even when reading out Golden Age texts) according to their own contemporary norms, and it was not until the 20th century that classical pronunciation was largely re-established in education (although the Italian pronunciation, known as *Lingua Latīna Ecclēsiastica* or "Ecclesiastical Latin", is still preferred by the Church and, mostly, in music).

Even then, aspects of that classical pronunciation remain contested, or indeed in recent decades have proven inaccurate. Some key points of agreement among current linguists include:

- from around 250 BC, word stress shifted from the first syllable typically to the penultimate or antepenultimate depending on the length of the vowel and consonant/vowel pattern of the penultimate syllable (although between this time and the Golden Age period there was also the loss of some final post-vocalic consonants and consequent lengthening of resultant final vowels which then led to some exceptions to this);
- as is often forgotten in education but now agreed by philologists, vowel length was essential (for example, ancient Romans viewed short [A] and long [Ā] as two different letters, even though they were based on the same pronunciation and generally written the same way);
- consonants were softer (less plosive) than in some modern languages such as English;

- the pair [I] and [J] were absolutely regarded as the same letter, as were [U] and [V]; and
- [M] and [N] generally caused preceding vowels to be nasalized (even though this is still rarely recognized in education).

Points still of minor contention include:
- [C] and [G] (originally regarded as the same letter but clearly distinguished by the Golden Age period) were always pronounced hard, but there is some evidence that before high vowels ([E], [I] and in practice by the Golden Age period also [AE] and [OE]) they were pronounced with a slight y-glide (the same effect as in English 'cube');
- English- and German-speaking linguists often posit a seven-vowel system (typically with [E] and [Ē], and [I] and [Ī] exhibiting not just distinct length but distinct quality) but this seems at odds with subsequent development and Southern European linguists generally assume only five (i.e. all five native vowels simply had long and short forms; [Y] was a sixth vowel but appeared only in borrowings from Greek);
- [V], while certainly closer to the pronunciation of English <w> than modern Italian <v>, may in fact have been somewhere between /ß/ (as in Spanish *vivir*) and /w/ rather than purely /w/ as is often taught, particularly when appearing between vowels;
- the third person form *est* 'is' and the conjunction *et* 'and' may have been strongly elided (i.e. to something approaching *'st* and *'t*) in speech (i.e. at all times, not just in poetry or colloquial speech), particularly after vowels and nasals; and
- in common speech, where a word ended in a vowel or a nasal, that final sound was often elided (by omission or conversion into a semi-vowel) if the next word began with a vowel or *h-*.

The result was a language from which harsher and slushier sounds (e.g. German <ch>, /x/; or English <sh>, /ʃ/) were entirely absent; however, it would have been markedly less vocalic than its daughter languages and, when read aloud, its rhythm sounds quite alien even to speakers of them. This is primarily because of Classical Latin's unstressed final syllables and frequent long vowels (as well as long consonants, retained among today's major national languages descended from it only in Italian). Late Latin, which distinguished previously long versus short vowels by quality rather than length and generally dropped final nasal consonants (3.1), would sound much more familiar to speakers of daughter languages, particularly Italian and Spanish.

There is, however, little doubt that Classical Latin was, like its daughter languages, pronounced forward in the mouth – this is a key point often overlooked in reconstructions of its pronunciation.

2.2   Standard

Before the age of printing or even paper (although they had *papyrus,* a word itself borrowed from Greek), the Romans did not require a written standard. However, ultimately, a form of Latin based significantly on the writings of Cicero and the oratory of Julius Caesar came to be recognized as "Classical" (understood to mean "first class"). This has been used among the educated and in schools ever since.

Educated Romans of Caesar's time and after were generally aware that their language had developed and changed through time and that there was an earlier version (typically referred to now as Early or "Archaic" Latin) which was generally intelligible but clearly distinct. Many knew that older grammatical inflections had in time been dropped or amended (such as ablative *-ad* or *-od,* which had become *-ā* and *-ō*), and that sound change had had an impact even on common words; in some cases, older forms remained in some contexts (for example, initial *du-* became *b-* over a period during the second or third century BC, so Early Latin *duenos* became Classical *bonus* 'good'; but the older *du-* was retained in more commonly used forms of the word in some cases, such as the number *duo* 'two', hence even modern English 'dual' but 'binary').

The Romans were not generally of the view that their Latin was in any way superior linguistically to that which had gone before or to any other language – indeed, if anything, the opposite applied as the upper classes often chose to speak to each other in what they regarded as the true language of high culture, namely Greek.

Latin was written with an alphabet ultimately derived from Phoenician, which extended by the Golden Age period to 23 still familiar letters. [K] was by some writers considered the same as [C]; [G] and [X] were borrowed from Greek during the Early Latin period; [Y] and [Z] were confined to words of Greek origin (initially so were the digraphs [CH], [PH], [RH] and [TH] to mark more aspirated consonants; consonants were softer in native Latin words); there was no U/V or I/J distinction and no [W]. Latin was largely written as spoken, although already by the Golden Age period [AE] and [OE] were merging even occasionally in educated speech to [E]. Some conservative orators, conversely, retained an Early Latin [O] where the Classical written form had become [U] (notably *equus* 'horse' was often pronounced as if **equos*).

In ancient times, Latin was written only in capitals. An acute mark, now more commonly a horizontal accent mark (e.g. [Ā]), was occasionally used to mark long vowels or even long consonants; long consonants were more usually marked by doubling.

2.3   Vocabulary

Key numbers:
I ūnus II duo III trēs IV quattuor V quīnque VI sex VII septem VIII octō IX novem;
X decem, XI ūndecim, XVI sēdecim, XVII septendecim, XVIII duodēvīgintī;
XX vīgintī, XI vīgintī ūnus; C centum; M mille.

Classical Latin still displayed vestiges of the old octal (base eight) counting system (1.3), as the last two numbers in each ten were typically reverse-counted (thus 19/*XIX ūndēvīgintī* '[one-from-twenty]'; very rarely *novemdecim* '[nine-ten]'); this applied all the way up (e.g 99/*XCIX ūndēcentum* 'one-from-hundred'). Later numbers could also be counted unit first (so 24/*XXIV* could be *vīgintī quattuor* 'twenty four' or *quattuor et vīgintī* '[four-and-twenty]').

Vocabulary was inherited largely from Proto-Indo-European, with additions from other languages spoken in the Italian peninsula. There were significant borrowings from Greek during the Golden Age; Greek influence also led to the greater use of compound words.

Personal pronouns:

	Singular (1st, 2nd person)		Plural (1st, 2nd person)	
Nominative	*ego*	*tū*	*nōs*	*vōs*
Accusative	*mē*	*tē*	*nōs*	*vōs*
Genitive	*meī*	*tuī*	*nostrum*	*vestrum*
Dative	*mihi*	*tibi*	*nōbis*	*vōbis*
Ablative	*mē*	*tē*	*nōbis*	*vōbis*

3rd person/demonstrative pronouns (masculine/feminine/neuter):

	Singular	Plural
Nominative	*is/ea/id*	*iī/eae/ea*
Accusative	*eum/eam/id*	*eōs/eās/ea*
Genitive	*eius*	*eōrum/eārum/eōrum*
Dative	*eī*	*eīs* or *iīs*
Ablative	*eō/eā/eō*	*eīs* or *iīs*

Third person pronouns were initially not present in the language as such, but by the time of Classical Latin were generally regarded as aligned grammatically with first and second person personal pronouns (despite a clearly distinct origin).

Demonstratives, likewise fully declined (2.4), are generally regarded to have exhibited three grades: *hic-haec-hoc* 'this, near me'; *iste-ista-istud* 'that, near you'; *ille-illa-illud* 'that, yonder'. Another demonstrative *ipse-ipsa-ipsum* was used effectively as a partial reflexive pronoun, but it also in some senses carried a demonstrative meaning of 'this, near you'. A further determiner *īdem-eadem-idem*, declined similarly to *is/ea/id* plus the ending *-dem*, carried the meaning of 'same'.

The relative pronoun series was *quī-quae-quod,* although these were much rarer than in modern languages, as alternative structures of expressing subordinate relationships were often preferred.

The interrogative pronoun *quis-quis-quid* in fact was otherwise declined exactly as *quī-quae-quod;* it stood alongside other specific pronouns such as *quandō* 'why, when', *cūr* 'why' and *ubi* 'where'.

2.4   Grammar

Latin is renowned for its complex grammar, but in fact even two millennia ago it was no more complex than what went before and was in many ways as straightforward as many modern languages such as Russian or even German.

Noun endings changed depending on grammatical case, of which there were in practice five (contrary to the commonly taught six) plus vestiges of two more, a decrease from Proto-Indo-European's eight or nine (1.4); most nouns fell into one of five declensions, which dictated the pattern by which they formed different cases. Nouns were also one of three genders, which dictated how adjective or determiner endings also changed to agree with them. Thus *ille puer* 'that boy', *illa puella* 'that girl', *illud vallum* 'that wall', *puer bonus* 'a good boy', *puella bona* 'a good girl', *vallum bonum* 'a good wall'; but also *illum puerum* 'that boy' (accusative; direct object), *illā puellā* '(by) that girl' (ablative), *illī vallī* '(to) that wall' (dative); *illōs puerōs* 'those boys' (accusative), *illārum puellārum* '(of) those girls' (genitive), etc; unfortunately, adjective and noun endings did not always match so neatly (e.g. *Italiā boreālī* 'from northern Italy', ablative).

Regular noun declension (*mēnsa* 'table'; *fundus* 'ground'; *rēx* 'king'; *manus* 'hand'; *rēs* 'thing'):

Singular	1st	2nd	3rd	4th	5th
Nominative	*mēnsa*	*fundus*	*rēx*	*manus*	*rēs*
Accusative	*mēnsam*	*fundum*	*rēgem*	*manum*	*rem*
Genitive	*mēnsae*	*fundī*	*rēgis*	*manūs*	*rēī*
Dative	*mēnsae*	*fundī*	*rēgī*	*manuī*	*rēī*
Ablative	*mēnsā*	*fundō*	*rēge*	*manū*	*rē*

Plural	1st	2nd	3rd	4th	5th
Nominative	*mēnsae*	*fundī*	*rēgēs*	*manūs*	*rēs*
Accusative	*mēnsās*	*fundōs*	*rēgēs*	*manūs*	*rēs*
Genitive	*mēnsārum*	*fundōrum*	*rēgum*	*manuum*	*rērum*
Dative	*mēnsīs*	*fundīs*	*rēgibus*	*manibus*	*rēbus*
Ablative	*mēnsīs*	*fundīs*	*rēgibus*	*manibus*	*rēbus*

Verbs were marked for tense/aspect (ranging from pluperfect to future), voice (active and medio-passive) and mood (indicative, subjunctive and imperative), mostly synthetically (i.e. by changing endings with occasional other modifications), with additional supine, gerunds (noun and adjectival forms) and various infinitive markers coded for voice and tense. They typically fell into one of four regular classes, but common verbs were often irregular.

The basic regular verb endings in the present tense are familiar even to speakers of modern languages derived from Latin (-*a*- stem; 1st, 2nd and 3rd person):

- sg. *cantō* 'I sing', *cantās* 'you sing', *cantat* 'he/she/it sings';
- pl. *cantāmus* 'we sing', *cantātis* 'you sing', *cantant* 'they sing'.

However, even a verb as simple as *cantāre* 'sing' could have over 100 more different forms (more than twice as many as even the most verbally complex modern Western European national language), among them:

- *cantābimus* 'we will sing' [future indicative active],
- *cantābant* 'they were singing' [imperfect indicative active],
- *cantāvistis* 'you [plural] sang' [perfect indicative active],
- *cantāverat* 'she had sung' [pluperfect indicative active],
- *cantātur* 'it is sung' [present indicative passive],
- *cantābantur* 'they were sung' [perfect indicative passive],
- *cantābitur* 'it will be sung' [future indicative passive],
- *cantēs* 'you [singular] may sing' [present subjunctive active],
- *cantārēmus* 'we may have been singing' [imperf. subj. act.],
- *cantāverint* 'they may have sung' [perfect subjuctive active],

- *cantāvissem* 'I may have sung before' [pluperf. subj. active],
- *cantētur* 'it may be sung' [present subjunctive passive],
- *cantārentur* 'they may have been sung' [perf. subj. passive].

Note the absence of a future subjunctive, even though there is one in modern Portuguese (8.4).

There was also the imperative:
- *cantā* 'sing!' [singular]
- *cantātōte* 'sing!' [plural]
- *cantātor* 'it shall be sung';

and infinitives:
- *cantāre* 'to sing',
- *cantāvisse* 'to have sung',
- *cantārī* 'to be sung';

plus gerund/participles:
- *cantandum* 'singing' [noun],
- *cantāns* 'singing' [adjective],
- *cantātus* 'sung' [participle].

Adjectives also had their own three declensions; with the first two, adverbs were formed by the suffix *-ē* or occasionally *-e* (*vērē* 'truly', *male* 'badly') and with the third by *-iter* (*fortiter* 'strongly'); some common adverbs maintained other modifications (e.g. *bene* 'well').

Notably, Classical Latin lacked articles (even though contemporary Greek had them) and, given its case endings already carried so much meaning, it made considerably less (and arguably more specific) use of prepositions than its daughter languages.

Latin word order in the Golden Age was most often SOV, though the preference for prepositions rather than postpositions suggests it was beginning to shift slowly towards SVO; however, it was much freer than in its daughter languages, with the predominant consideration not word class but emphasis. The most common negative particle, typically placed directly before the verb, was *nōn* (although common verbs had their own negative forms: *volō* 'I want', *nolō* 'I do not want'); other means of expressing negation, including via negative conjunctions (e.g. *nec/neque*), were also common. Not only could clauses be ordered more or less as the speaker/author desired, but due to agreement of adjectives/determiners and nouns elements could even be separated – *magnam* vidi nocte in caelō *stellam* 'I saw a big star in the sky by night' / 'Big was the star that I saw in the night sky'.

Yes/no questions required the suffix *-ne*:
- *cantat* 'she sings'; *cantatne?* 'does she sing?'

Answer:
- affirmative *sīc* 'thus, yes', *ita* 'thus', *cantat* '(yes) she sings';
- negative *nōn cantat* 'she does not sing', *minimē!* 'no way!'

2.5   Character

To modern readers, Classical Latin is instantly recognizable and thus weirdly familiar, and yet at the same time quite alien. The way words are marked and clauses are constructed requires an entirely different thought process from that used for the most widely spoken modern Western European languages; and the sound and rhythm of the language, particularly with its distinctive word stress and the frequency of long vowels and consonants, are very strange to modern ears.

It is worth emphasizing that it is not Classical but Late Latin (Chapter 3), itself derived directly from Vulgar Latin, which is the direct ancestor of modern Italic (or Romance) languages. The structure of Late Latin, as well as its grammar, phonology and vocabulary, give it an instantly more familiar character. Given it is closer in every way to the modern day, it is Late Latin which would be more relevant to contemporary language learning, all other things being equal.

Of course, because of Classical Latin's literary prestige, all other things are not equal. Unfamiliar though it looks and odd though it sounds, the echoes of Classical Latin are with us every hour of every day. Indeed, the classical language (with some neologisms) is still perfectly capable of being used in the modern world, in speech as well as in writing. Its study at once opens a window to our collective heritage, but also to linguistics in general and thus to language learning of any kind. Learning Classical Latin is in some ways like getting to know a family member we have just met and did not previously know existed – sometimes it is frustrating or even bizarre, and yet there is a strand of familiarity which profoundly connects us.

Classical Latin, of course, did not stop at one point in time as a language in spoken use, even if it did as a written classical language. Already by the Golden Age or soon after it is apparent that, among other changes, some (predominantly but not exclusively uneducated rural) speakers were:

- levelling [AE] and [OE] to merge with [E] (2.1);
- then also shifting [I] to [E];
- switching short [O] and [U];
- vocalizing [AL] to [AU] and then shifting this also to [O];
- simplifying consonant clusters (e.g. *ipse* > *esse*); and
- dropping medial nasal consonants after vowels (*mēnsa* > *mesa*).

Generally, that predominantly rural form of spoken Latin was the one taken by the legionaries (who were themselves often second-language speakers) to Iberia and is thus the basis for Spanish, while the educated more conservative form maintained greater influence in Italy (cf. Spanish *otra lengua* versus Italian *altra lingua* 'other language' – although these examples represent a tendency, not a universal). The case system also came under pressure both from the merger of vowel combinations and the elision of case endings (2.4), and so prepositions were notably more common by the fourth century even in writing, often broadening their meaning (e.g. modern *de/di* derives from the Latin *dē* 'about, concerning, from', but came to encompass 'of, belonging to').

Across what was the Western Roman Empire, speakers of daughter dialects all regarded themselves as "Latin" speakers until at least the end of the seventh century. However, by the middle of the eighth century in modern-day France it was becoming impossible for speakers of the local vernacular to understand even simple Church readings in Latin; by the ninth century it is recorded that diplomatic missions became difficult because Latin was so different across the continent; by the end of the first millennium no one anywhere (even in the Italian peninsula itself) was in any doubt that the local vernacular speech constituted a clearly different language from the Latin of the Church. The story of the modern "Romance" Languages had thus begun.

Pater noster quī es in caelīs, sanctificētur nōmen tuum; adveniat regnum tuum; fiat voluntās tua; sīcut in caelō et in terrā; pānem nostrum cotīdiānum dā nōbis hodiē; et dīmitte nōbis dēbita nostra; sīcut et nōs dīmittimus dēbitōribus nostrīs; et nē nōs indūcās in tentātiōnem; sed līberā nōs ā malō.

3

VULGAR LATIN

As most people with even a passing interest in languages know, what are referred to today as "Romance" languages are all derived from Latin. There is an understandable tendency, therefore, to compare the likes of Portuguese, Spanish, French and Italian to the form of Latin spoken and written when it was at its most prestigious (Chapter 2).

However, despite dialectal variation, Latin remained a single, coherent spoken language for many centuries afterwards. Even well into the second half of the first millennium, it was possible for travellers anywhere in western or southern Europe or even north Africa to use Latin to communicate. However, the Latin language after the fall of Rome was as distant in time from Cicero as Modern English is from Chaucer. Not only was there the natural process of language change which had occurred during this period, but also the reality that the form of the language which emerged through the centuries was not derived from the classical language written in literary works, but from the colloquial language spoken in the streets and farms (2.5).

Purely linguistically, therefore, it is this colloquial, spoken form to which comparisons can most usefully be made to help the study of modern languages. In fact, it is a reasonable estimate that around half the changes which took place between Classical Latin and modern Portuguese, Spanish, French and Italian had already occurred before they split to become identifiably distinct local languages. Therefore this later version, based on colloquial or "Vulgar" Latin but perhaps more accurately defined as "Late" Latin, is surely worthy of some focus.

3.1   Phonology

The phonological changes between Classical and Late Latin had a considerable impact on the grammar and character of the language.

Some of those changes were already occurring in colloquial speech even early in the Roman Empire, most notably perhaps the loss of final post-vocalic <m>. Long and short vowels also ceased to be contrastive early in the first millennium. All of this meant that the distinction between, for example, *mēnsa* (subject), *mēnsam* (object) and *mēnsā* (ablative, 'by') was already largely lost in speech.

In most dialects there was significant palatization of consonants (in effect, the subtle pronunciation of a sound written in English as <y> after the consonant itself) in some positions, particularly before high vowels (usually written <i> or <e>). The most notable instances were /k/ (usually written <c> across Italic languages) and /g/; it also affected /t/, giving it a sound more like /ts/ before high vowels (thus Classical Latin *grātiae*, modern Italian *grazie* 'thanks'). The exact outcome of this palatization in different dialects varied (and some insular dialects avoided the change altogether).

The letter <v> moved from the Classical pronunciation close to /w/ to close to the more modern sounding /v/. The old aspirated consonants, written <ph>, <th> and <ch>, were not pronounced separately from /f/, /t/ and /k/ in colloquial usage anyway, and soon merged with them in speech; /h/ standing alone was dropped altogether.

Even though the location of articulation towards the front of the mouth was likely the same, stress became more marked than in Classical Latin, which may have been more pitch-based. Along with the practical loss of distinction between long and short vowels, numerous unstressed syllables were lost, and various consonant clusters became simplified (sometimes in different ways in different dialects). This meant Late Latin had a considerably more even syllable length and a more vocalic sound than Classical Latin, although still not as markedly as Modern Italian (7.1).

3.2   Standard

Most Late Latin speakers remained illiterate, although a sizeable minority could read and write. However, what they read and wrote, until somewhere between the late seventh and ninth century depending on location, was Classical Latin (2.2). Speakers would have been aware that there was a marked distinction between the way they spoke and the way they wrote, but also that the classical written form was essential to understanding in education and the Church. From the late first millennium, intelligibility began to break down completely and local vernaculars began the process of developing into recognizably distinct tongues and appearing in writing. Some of these ultimately formed the basis for the standard versions of daughter languages such as Italian (7.2), Portuguese (8.2), Spanish (9.2) and French (10.2).

3.3   Vocabulary

Key numbers:

I unu, II duu, III tres, IV quattuor, V cinque, VI ses, VII septe, VIII octu, IX nove;
X dece, XI undeci, XVI sedeci, XVII septedeci, XVIII octudeci;
XX veinti, XXI veinti unu; C centu; M mil.

Vocabulary remained overwhelmingly from Early Latin; Greek influence was markedly less evident in western dialects than it was in the east even in the Classical period. Over time some words were lost as others expanded their meaning (e.g. Early and Classical Latin *caballus*, originally itself a non-Indo-European borrowing, specifically meant 'nag'; but by Late Latin *caballu* meant 'horse', thus Classical *equus* was lost in some dialects and narrowed in meaning in others).

Personal pronouns:

	Singular (1st, 2nd)		Plural (1st, 2nd)	
Subject	*eo*	*tu*	*nos*	*vos*
Object	*me*	*te*		
Possessive	*mei*	*tui*	*nostru*	*vostru*

Except in eastern dialects, direct and indirect object forms were no longer distinguished in the first and second person (although fuller forms, which ultimately came to be used primarily after prepositions, were developing). However, third person forms *ille-illa* (the subject forms of which were also adopted as the definite article) were still distinguished between direct object (singular *illu-illa*) and indirect object (singular *illi*); plural forms varied between dialects.

Demonstrative forms derived from *este-esta* 'this, that' (Classical *iste-ista*); relative and interrogative pronouns from *qui* 'what, that', alongside *quando* 'when', *ube* 'where', *quomo* 'how'.

3.4   Grammar

In theory, nouns retained a three-gender system (though neuter nouns typically merged with masculine over time) as well as their declension system of five groupings determined primarily by their stem vowel. However, because of phonological changes (3.1) plus, in some northern dialects, Germanic influence, distinctions between the five core noun cases of Classical Latin were lost, regardless of declension. Initially these were reduced and then, in some dialects, extinguished altogether; for example (using 'table'), *mēnsa-mēnsam-mēnsae-mēnsae-mēnsā* became simply *mesa-mesa-mese-mese-mesa,* thus distinguished only between a "general" case *mesa* on one hand and a combined "possessive/indirect object" *mese* on the other; similarly (though initially not quite identically) Classical *fundus-fundum-fundī-fundī-fundō* 'ground' became in effect just *fondu-fondi*. Ultimately, this was reduced to one singular form in most (though not all) dialects, usually based on the accusative (the singular object form which, in Classical Latin, usually ended in *-m*). Plural forms varied along a broad west/east split – typically western dialects also adopted the accusative (object) plural form for all cases (*mesas, fondos*); in eastern dialects it was more complex as they effectively maintained the nominative (subject) plural form for all cases (*mese, fondi*); and there were some exceptions (some northern dialects maintained *-s* endings on masculine nouns specifically to mark singular subject or plural object; some eastern dialects maintained a separate possessive/indirect object form).

Verbs remained marked primarily for tense; as well as for voice and mood, but there was a significant shift towards using auxiliary verbs rather than endings to mark these:

- the present tense remained a single tense marked almost exactly as in Classical Latin;
- the past tense retained a distinction between imperfect and perfect action (i.e. repeated/continuous action or single action), but endings were shortened;
- a present perfect construction, consisting of the verb *abere* 'have' or *essere* 'be' followed by a past participle (e.g. *cantatu* 'sung'), originally marked a past action affecting the present, but came to be used in some dialects to refer to a single action in the past (and, with the imperfect rather than present form of *abere* or *essere*, this construction began to take over entirely as the pluperfect in most dialects);
- future forms were abandoned but a new verb form using the infinitive (e.g. *cantare* 'sing') combined with the endings of the verb *abere* came into use, initially as a future perfect;
- an additional near future tense was formed from *ire* 'go' with the infinitive (*vas cantare* 'you are going to sing') – in eastern dialects, this form took over completely as the future;
- the imperative (ordering) and subjunctive (counter-factual) moods were retained, the latter in present and past tenses (although past forms became unstable and were eventually merged with the pluperfect);
- passive verb forms were lost, replaced by a construction with *essere* and the past participle (*es cantatu* 'it is sung') or more commonly by a simple reflexive (*se cantat*); and
- in clause construction, there was considerably less dependence on infinitives coded for tense or on gerunds.

In Classical and Late Latin, as in Modern Spanish, *canto* on its own meant 'I sing', *cantas* 'you sing', and so on – a grammatical feature known as "pro-drop". This feature was also shared by Germanic languages at the time (4.4), but it no longer applies to any modern Germanic language; it was also lost in French in the 13th century (10.4).

Verb endings of *cantare* 'sing', (*-a-* stem; 1st, 2nd, 3rd person).

Present indicative ('sing'):
- singular *canto, cantas, canta(t);*
- plural *cantamus, cantates, cantan(t).*

Present subjunctive:
- singular *cante, cantes, cante(t);*
- plural *cantemus, cantetes, canten(t).*

Imperfect indicative ('used to sing'):
- singular *cantaba, cantabas, cantaba(t);*
- plural *cantabamus, cantabates, cantaban(t).*

Imperfect subjunctive:
- singular *cantare, cantares, cantare(t);*
- plural *cantaremus, cantaretes, cantaren(t).*

Pluperfect indicative ('had sung'):
- singular *cantara, cantaras, cantara(t);*
- plural *cantaramus, cantarates, cantaran(t).*

Pluperfect subjunctive:
- singular *cantasse, cantasses, cantasse(t);*
- plural *cantassemus, cantassetes, cantassen(t).*

Preterite/Perfect ('sang/have sung'):
- singular *cantai, cantasti, cantau(t);*
- plural *cantammus, cantastes, cantarun(t).*

Future perfect ('will have sung'):
- singular *cantare, cantares, cantare(t);*
- plural *cantaremus, cantaretes, cantaren(t).*

There was also the imperative (singular *canta*, plural *cantate*); past participle *cantatu*; present participle *cantante;* and gerund *cantandu.*

The *-t* of third person endings was gradually lost during the Late Latin period, except perhaps in some northern dialects.

The future perfect was distinguished from the imperfect subjunctive by stress on a later (typically final rather than penultimate) syllable; the latter was eventually replaced entirely in all dialects.

These future perfect endings, developed as an innovation from Vulgar Latin, ultimately came to represent the simple future; this innovation did not occur in eastern and insular dialects, however, from which future endings were simply absent.

Adjectives continued to agree with nouns in gender, number and case. They tended to be placed after the noun when used attributively (but this was not compulsory). Gradually from the first century, however, adverbs came to be formed by adding the suffix *mente* 'with mind', derived from the ablative form of a feminine noun: *lentu* 'slow, tedious', feminine *lenta*, adverb *lentamente* 'with slow mind, slowly, tediously'; some common adverbs such as *bene* 'well' and *male* 'badly' did not follow this pattern and became outright irregular. Classical comparative endings disappeared, replaced by constructions with *plus* or *magis* 'more' (tending towards the latter farther west).

However, perhaps the most obvious difference from Classical was the explosion in prepositions, and the introduction of articles. Because nouns were no longer so clearly marked for case, prepositions were required to establish meaning – so words such as *de, ad* and *com* came into much wider use, although not quite always strictly as prepositions (*com* in particular was generally used as a postposition with pronouns – *tecom* 'with you' [you-with]). For the same reason, the determiner *ille/illa/illu* 'that' expanded in meaning to appear in front of nouns widely, thus generally translated as the definite article 'the' (as well as being adopted as third person pronouns in most dialects; 3.3); and the numeral *un(us)/una/unu* 'one' expanded to become the indefinite article 'a/an'.

The subordinating conjunction *que* (developed from Classical *quid/quod*), which ultimately came to be pronounced without the /w/ sound, came into more common use during the Late Latin period.

Word order shifted in Late Latin from the SOV of Classical to SVO (though SOV was retained where the object was a pronoun); however, VSO was preferred when the verb expressed motion or change of state.

SVO or VSO were possible for questions. The Classical negative particle *non* was retained but its use was much more widespread, with other negative conjunctions and particles lost or restricted.

Yes/no questions began to rely merely on intonation, sometimes (in the west and north) with an additional phrase *es(t) quod* 'is it that':
- *canta(t)* 'she sings';
- *canta(t)? / es(t) quod canta(t)?* 'does she sing?'

Answer *sic* 'yes'; *non* 'no'.

3.5   Character

Late Latin was of Latin-Faliscan origin but, unlike the Classical Latin of the Golden Age period, it was spoken at a time when all other Italic languages had been lost.

It was markedly more vocalic and verb-focused than Classical. Many complex constructions around nouns were replaced through the Late Latin period by clauses centring on verbs.

For its entire existence, bar the odd inscription, "Vulgar" Latin remained a solely spoken language (all the forms given here are reconstructed rather than attested). Nevertheless, its structures and basic character look instantly more modern. While it may understandably lack the literary prestige of what went before or what came after, it is this version of Latin which is the direct ancestor of languages spoken and written by hundreds of millions of people across the world today.

Patre nostru, qui es in illi celi, santificetu es tuu nome. Adveniat tuu regnu. Es tua volunta, sic quomo in ille celu et in illa terra. Nostru pane quotidianu danos hoie, et nos dimitte nostra debita sic quomo nos dimittimus illi debitori nostri. Et non nos induce in illa tentatione, mae nos libere de ille malu.

4

GOTHIC

Gothic is important because it provides the earliest clear attestation of a Germanic language. That attestation comes from the fourth century, and therefore from a period which can reasonably be described as close to the middle of the transition from Classical Latin (Chapter 2) to Late Latin (Chapter 3). It therefore enables us to draw a parallel between historical Germanic (the current forms of which are represented mainly by German, Dutch, the Nordic languages and of course English) and Latinate (now including Italian, Portuguese, Spanish and French) as they were at roughly the same point in time.

The parallel is, unfortunately, not exact. Gothic was an East Germanic language, and in fact has no surviving daughter languages. Nevertheless, it would have been largely mutually intelligible with West and North Germanic languages, and it shared many distinct Germanic features in common with them.

It is also useful because it is attested in a Bible translation (carried out in Constantinople), which makes precise understanding easier. The emerging view from recent studies that this translation was the work of a team of scholars (rather than just one bishop, Wulfilas, as previously thought) only enhances its linguistic value.

4.1 Phonology

Gothic was, fundamentally, not unlike Vulgar Latin phonologically, but with a lot more fricatives (/f/, /v/) rather than plosives (/p/, /b/).

Otherwise, Gothic and Latin had similar sets of consonants and vowels, and Gothic also happened to have three diphthongs (Gothic's were <ai>, <au> and <iu>, with the emphasis on the first letter). In Gothic, the pronunciation of consonants written <d>, <t> and possibly also <b> was much softer in certain contexts, in some instances close to the modern English pronunciation of <th>. Unlike modern Germanic languages, but like Latin, Gothic had nasal sounds (often in fact written <gg>); <l>, <m>, <n> and <r> could also serve as semi-vowels in clusters (*fugls* 'bird', *táikns* 'token').

The biggest distinction from Latin, however, concerned not sound but intonation. Stress in Gothic generally fell on the first syllable of the word; Classical Latin had moved this, typically to the penultimate or antepenultimate (2.1). Thus, in terms of intonation, Gothic and Latin would have sounded significantly different. Another difference, which perhaps arose from this, was that Gothic almost certainly maintained a glottal stop before words beginning with a vowel, whereas Latin did not.

Gothic consonants were devoiced at the end of a word (as with most dialects of German today; 13.2), but there was no sign yet of rhoticism (switching from /s/ to /r/, which occurred in all other Germanic languages: cf. English 'lo<u>s</u>t' versus 'forlo<u>rn</u>'; 'wa<u>s</u>' versus 'we<u>r</u>e').

It is impossible to know exactly what the place of articulation was for Gothic, nor exactly how stress was applied (in theory Gothic could even have been tonal, although there is no direct evidence that it was).

4.2　Standard

Gothic had no standard form as such, and most of its speakers were illiterate. However, written forms are taken from remaining fragments of the Bible translation; in linguistic study, this forms a retrospective "standard" version of the language. One slight drawback to this is that it is, by definition, a translation (from Greek); this means it gives us few hints as to the colloquial or even natural spoken language.

4.3   Vocabulary

Vocabulary was almost entirely Germanic, but this meant it was not always Indo-European – some linguists suggest as much as a third of Germanic vocabulary is of a different origin.

Key numbers:
1 áins, 2 twái, 3 þrija, 4 fidwōr, 5 fimf, 6 saíhs, 7 sibun, 8 ahtáu, 9 niun;
10 taíhun, 11 áinlif, 12 twalif, 16 saíhstaíhun, 17 sibuntaíhun;
20 twái tigjus, 60 saíhs tigjus, 70 sibuntēhund;
100 taíhuntēhund, 200 twá(i) hunda, 100 þūsundi;
456789 fidwōr hunda saíhsuhfimf tigjus þūsundjos sibun hunda
niunuhahtáutēhund.

4.4   Grammar

Gothic maintained the Indo-European declension system (where noun endings were different according to groupings determined by the final vowel), which was also retained to an extent even in Late Latin (3.4) but in fact was probably already largely lost by this time in other Germanic languages (which retained merely a "strong" and "weak" declension). Nouns displayed three genders and four cases (as in modern Standard German and Icelandic), but also three numbers (including dual, which was sporadically used in Ancient Greek but was absent even from Early Latin).

Unlike modern Germanic languages, but like Latin and most languages descended from it, Gothic was in fact "pro-drop", meaning verbs could stand alone without a subject (because endings of verbs already clearly indicated person).

As in Latin, Gothic verbs agreed with their subject in person (I, you, he/she/it, etc) and number, although it appears there were no distinct third person dual forms. Endings or changes to the root vowel could mark one of two voices (active or middle/passive) or three moods (indicative; optative, effectively now subjunctive/conjunctive; or imperative). Infinitives, present participles or past passive forms could be turned into nouns. Where Gothic verbs were notably different from Latin was that they were only directly marked for two tenses, past and present (or "not past") – a significant comparative simplification. Gothic verbs were either "strong" (forming their past by way of a vowel change: e.g. *bindan* 'to bind', *band* 'bound') or "weak" (forming their past essentially by adding *-d* or *-t*); this division is maintained in all Germanic languages to the present day, although the number of strong verbs has declined considerably (Gothic had perhaps as many as five times as many strong verbs as modern English or German).

The Gothic verb *sōkja* 'seek', in the present active indicative (1st, 2nd, 3rd person):
- Singular *sōkja, sōkjis, sōkjiþ*;
- Dual *sōkjōs, sōkjats;*
- Plural *sōkjam, sōkjaiþ, sōkjand.*

Adjectives agreed with nouns for case, gender and number. The division in later Germanic languages between "weak" and "strong" endings was not yet apparent.

As with Latin, Gothic made use of clitics to mark whether a question was being asked – Gothic *-u* was equivalent to Latin *-ne*. These were lost in all other Germanic languages.

There is some dispute over Gothic word order, which was relatively free but seemingly essentially still SOV.

Key personal pronouns in Gothic (1st, 2nd person; nominative/accusative/genitive/dative case):
- Singular: *ik/mik/meina/mis; þu/þuk/þeina/þus.*
- Dual: *wit/ugkis/igkara/ugkis; jut/igqis/igqara/igqis.*
- Plural: *weis/uns/unsara/uns; jus/izwis/izwara/izwis.*

3rd person also existed with singular and plural in all genders (but seemingly not dual).

4.5   Character

It is hard to assess the character of Gothic, as almost all we have of it is a religious translation.

Assessing the language as it was used in daily speech is further complicated by the fact those who spoke it travelled widely, and so there were doubtless many variants of it. However, that did mean they left their mark on languages across the continent. In many locations including parts of what are now Spain, Italy and France, Gothic was once spoken but gave way ultimately to Vulgar Latin (Chapter 3).

The most notable mark left by the Goths on Latin-derived languages was perhaps in Spain, particularly regarding names. Common Spanish (and thus Latin American) surnames such as *Ruiz, González* and *Fernández* are in fact all derived from Gothic. The word *rico* 'rich', which of course also appears in the names *Costa Rica* and *Puerto Rico*, is likewise a Gothic borrowing. Here we see a classic example of how ancient connections between Germanic languages and Latin continue to resonate globally today.

Although clearly Germanic (and displaying many of the sound shifts which typify it), Gothic was remarkably conservative phonologically and grammatically, probably more so than unattested contemporary Germanic languages to the north and west.

Atta unsar þu in himinam, weihnai namo þein, qimai þiudinassus þeins, wairþai wilja þeins, swe in himina jah ana airþai. Hlaif unsarana þana sinteinan gif uns himma daga, jah aflet uns þatei skulans sijaima, swaswe jah weis afletam þaim skulam unsaraim, jah ni briggais uns in fraistubnjai, ak lausei uns af þamma ubilin.

5

MIDDLE ENGLISH

It is sometimes worth pausing in our language learning journey to look at our own language as it once was, particularly when the story is as fascinating as that of English.

It seems astonishing now, but English just before the Black Death of the mid 14th century was a colloquial language of low status. The administrative and high language of England was Norman French, and the ecclesiastical and academic language was Latin. Furthermore, English was spoken only in England and parts of Wales; the language descending from Anglo-Saxon (also known as Old English) in Scotland was recognized as a separate language, Scots.

So, although "Middle English" linguistically covers the period from the Norman Conquest of the late 11th century to the invention of the printing press in the late 15th, written evidence of it comes almost exclusively from the last century or so of that period. The Black Death changed everything because it was devastating and indiscriminate; the largely French-speaking aristrocracy suffered just like everyone else. As survivors moved up the social scale in many instances to take their place, so did English; English was used in Parliament for the first time in 1362. Within decades, English also had Geoffrey Chaucer as a major literary figure. This, combined with the rise of English nationalism due to ongoing wars with France, confirmed its status as the national language. The rest of the rise, from national language to predominant global status, is history.

5.1 Phonology

We know a lot about the pronunciation of Chaucer and his contemporaries because the bizarre linguistic truth is that written Standard English today is based on the pronunciation of Middle English, not Modern English. This means a word like *name* was once pronounced exactly as it looks (and as it still is in modern German), though the <e> had become silent in all but the most careful speech by the 15th century. Words such as *night* were also losing the middle consonant sound (close to /x/ as in German *Na**ch**t*) in Chaucer's time. In words such as *write, knife* or *gnat*, the initial /w/, /k/ and /g/ were all still sounded; as was the /l/ in *talk*. Initial *wh-* was consistently fully pronounced; thus, the initial sound in *what* and *who* was identical.

Anglo-Saxon regarded the pair /f/ and /v/ as a single letter, and likewise the pair /s/ and /z/ (the distinction was only brought in by the influence of Norman French); these continued to be variously pronounced around the country and thus still used in writing interchangeably by scribes in some areas. Scribes also used /v/ and /u/ interchangeably, regarding them as absolutely the same letter (as in Classical Latin; 2.1).

During the Middle English period, there began one of the most debated examples among linguists of language change, known as the "Great Vowel Shift". Over a period of three centuries, this changed the pronunciation of all long vowels in English. This in large part explains the apparently deviant nature of modern English spelling.

Early Middle English also retained the letter "yogh" <ȝ>, which is usually (but by no means always) now <gh>; it was pronounced somewhere between /g/ and /j/ before high vowels (/e/, /i/ etc), but more like a hard /x/ (as in Scottish 'lo**ch**') otherwise. It also initially retained the letter "thorn" <Þ>, which was gradually replaced by <th>.

Middle English was probably pronounced towards the back of the mouth, and with stressed syllables strengthened and lengthened as in the modern language. It is just possible that this was slightly different at the time for words borrowed from French or Latin, where stress may have been more even.

5.2   Standard

In the Middle English period, variations in spelling and usage were widespread, depending on geographical origin, time, or even simply wanting to fit onto the page or the line. People even wrote their own name variously. This mattered less, as fewer people were literate.

A "chancery standard", in effect spellings to be used by the early civil service, did develop from the 15th century onwards as writing spread due to the increased availability of parchment. However, widespread standardization only occurred after the invention of the printing press into what is regarded as the (Early) Modern English period.

5.3   Vocabulary

Key numbers (though Roman Numerals in fact remained in use):
1 one, 2 tuo/twei, 3 thri, 4 fower, 5 five, 6 six, 7 sevene, 8 eight, 9 nyne;
10 ten, 11 ellevene, 12 twelve, 16 sixtene, 17 seventene;
20 twenty, 24 fower-and-twenty; 100 hundred; 1000 thowsand;
456789 fower hundred six-and-fifty thowsand sevene hundred nyne-and-eighty;
    or *fower hundred six-and-fifty thowsand sevene hundred fourscore-and-nyne.*

One was pronounced as written, to rhyme with 'alone'; *tuo* (specifically an old feminine form) came to predominate for 'two'.

The *score* (i.e. twenty), a word and a system borrowed from North Germanic (cf. Danish 12.3; also Norman influence on French, 10.3), was more frequently used in counting than in the modern language.

Ordinal numbers generally added *-the,* but they displayed some clearly irregular forms: *first* (a Germanic word); *second* (borrowed from French); *thridde* 'third'; *ferthe* 'fourth'.

Vocabulary was similarly mixed between Latinate (French and Latin) and Germanic origin as now, although there was probably greater awareness of the distinction (the oldest known song in the English language, *Sumer is icumen in* 'Summer has arrived', dates from early Middle English, but its vocabulary is exclusively Germanic).

Personal pronouns (masculine/feminine/impersonal):

	Singular (1st, 2nd, 3rd)			Plural (1st, 2nd, 3rd)		
Subject	*I*	*Þu, thou*	*he/sche/hit*	*we*	*ye*	*heo, they*
Oblique	*me*	*Þe, thee*	*him/hir/hit*	*us*	*you*	*hem, them*
Poss.	*mine*	*Þin, thine*	*his/hir/his*	*oure*	*youre*	*hire*

Pronouns maintained a distinction between the singular *Þu* (later *thou;* object *Þe/thee*) and plural *ye* (object *you*). Singular possessive forms came to be distinguished between *mine/thine* (the original forms, used latterly only before vowels or *h*-) and *my/thy* (used before other consonants) – cf. usage even in Modern English of the indefinite article *an/a*.

5.4   Grammar

Nouns had largely lost the Anglo-Saxon case system. However, the possessive remained, usually written *-(e)s* although there were exceptions. The plural had also settled on the ending *-(e)s*, but with numerous irregular plural forms in common use (e.g. *namen* 'names').

Verbs agreed with their subject and had a wider range of endings with which to do so. There were more "strong" verbs (marking past forms by vowel change rather than an ending) than in the modern language; e.g. *help-halp-iholpen* (which is regular in the modern language) stood alongside *sing-sang-isungen* (which is still irregular). The prefix *i-* (or sometimes *y-*, cf. German/Dutch *ge-*) to mark participles was lost in most but not all dialects by the end of the Middle English period.

Present of *liken* 'like' and *singen* 'sing' (1st, 2nd, 3rd person):
- Sg. *I like/sing, thou likest/singest, he/sche/hit liketh/singeth*;
- Pl. *we liken/singen, ye liken/singen, they liken/singen.*

Imperative was *like/sing* (singular), *liketh/singeth* (plural). Gerund was *likynge/singynge*; present participle *(i)likand/singand;* past participle *(i)liked* but *(i)sungen*. The gerund gradually took over from the present participle, initially in southern dialects.

Past of weak verb *liken* 'like' (1st, 2nd, 3rd person):
- Sg. *I likede, thou likedst, he/sche/hit likede;*
- Pl. *we likeden, ye likeden, they likeden.*

Past of strong verb *singen* 'sing' (1st, 2nd, 3rd person):
- Sg. *I sang, thou songe, he/sche/hit sang;*
- Pl. *we songen, ye songen, they songen.*

Adjectives only agreed with nouns by adding the ending *-e* after the definite article, a possessive, or in the plural (but not otherwise): *his longe name* 'his long name', *longe namen* 'long names', but *a long name* 'a long name'. Comparison settled on the endings *-er* and *-est* as in the modern language, although these could be affixed to any adjective regardless of length and could be supported for emphasis by the adverbs *more* and *moste*; occasionally they also caused other alterations in the adjective (*long-lenger* 'long-longer'; *greet-gretter* 'great-greater'). Adverbs were beginning to be distinguished from adjectives, generally by the ending *-liche* (irregular comparative ending *-loker*), often reduced to *-lie*.

Prepositions were broadly the same as in the modern language, but there were also specific combined forms with adverbs of place (*her* 'here', *thare* 'there') which were in much wider use: *hence* 'from here'; *whider* 'to where'; *wherefor* 'what for, why'. One noteworthy preposition since lost was *umbe* 'around' (cf. German *um*).

Word order was predominantly SVO, and VSO in questions (or after negative adverbs), although there were notable exceptions; the participle of any verb phrase often went to the end in subordinate clauses (*whan he hath hire name sungen* 'when he has sung their name'). Negation was predominantly by addition of the particle *nat* after the verb; *he singeth nat* 'he does not sing'. This could be supported by a pre-verbal particle *ne* for emphasis (effectively meaning double negation reinforced the negative): *he ne singeth nouȝt* 'he does not sing anything [he-not-sings-nothing]'.

Modal verbs (*can, shall* etc) could be used as full verbs, i.e. they could take an object: *I can musick* 'I can play music'.

However, a marked difference from the modern language was that the word *do* could only be used as a full verb – it had no auxiliary function (and therefore played no role in negation, emphasis or question formation).

One result of this was that, unlike in the modern language, yes/no questions were formed by simple inversion:
- *sche singeth* 'she sings'; *singeth sche?* 'does she sing?'

Answer *yea* 'yes', *no* 'no'; *yes* 'yes [in response to negative]'.

5.5   Character

Middle English was more quintessentially Germanic in character than the modern language, but much less so than Anglo-Saxon had been.

Regional and local dialects varied from each other just as they do in the modern language but, quite unlike modern "BBC English", Middle English was almost certainly spoken with a rising intonation everywhere. It would also have been more vocalic than the modern language (particularly early in the period when final <e> was still generally pronounced).

Fader oure that art in heuene, halewed be þi name: come þi kyngdom: fulfild be þi wil in heuene as in erþe: oure ech day bred ȝef us to day, and forȝeue us oure dettes as we forȝeuen to oure detoures: and ne led us nouȝt in temptacion, bote deliuere us of euel.

6

ESPERANTO

"Learn Esperanto first" is the name of a movement which recommends language learners start with what is supposedly the simplest widely spoken language in the world – albeit one whose natural development is restricted to the comparatively brief period since its construction in the late 19th century. Whether or not we accept this premise, there is little question that Esperanto, created effectively as a regularized merger of Germanic, Latinate and Slavic languages, is at least worth considering by anyone looking to broaden their linguistic horizons.

Esperanto was founded with the *pracelo* ('original goal') of becoming a "universal" language to improve international communication and thus international understanding. In that regard, it is frequently dismissed as a "failure", and it also suffers from some now outdated assumptions within its vocabulary and grammatical structure. Nevertheless, it is the most successful constructed language in history, with a vibrant global community of speakers into the present day. Most of all, it offers a fascinating insight into linguistics generally and into language learning specifically.

6.1   Phonology

Esperanto adheres to a fundamental rule that each letter has the same pronunciation, regardless of position. It is dubious whether this can be achieved in practice, but nevertheless it does make Esperanto easier to read (and write) than most natural languages.

For most learners, Esperanto's accented letters (the most common of which are <ĉ>, <ĝ>, <ĵ> and <ŝ>, but often in fact written <cx>, <gx>, <jx> and <sx> and pronounced respectively as in English 'church', 'geography', 'pleasure', 'shop') are the trickiest to distinguish and use. Also, <c> can catch out many learners, pronounced as if <ts> (in violation of another fundamental rule that there should be "one letter, one sound"). English speakers also need to note that, from their point of view, <j> is pronounced as if <y>.

Esperanto's rhythm varies depending on the native language of the speaker; some suggest that it should sound something like Italian, in which case articulation is well forward in the mouth and stress involves strengthening but not lengthening of the penultimate syllable.

6.2   Standard

The language has a "standard" or "fundamental" form based on the work of its founder, L. L. Zamenhof, and specifically his work known as the *Fundamento* published in Russian in what is now Poland in 1887.

An Academy in effect protects this standard form and applies it to new words (and technology) as required. In practice, some grammatical variation is permitted and vocabulary has broadened considerably.

6.3   Vocabulary

Esperanto's vocabulary is mainly Latinate (usually directly from Latin, *pluvi* 'rain', *vidi* 'see'; or from French, *grava* 'important', *preskau* 'almost'; but also from other languages such as Spanish, *almenau* 'at least'; Italian, *ankau* 'also'; or just general, *granda* 'big'), with a significant minority from Germanic (from English, *jes* 'yes', *birdo* 'bird'; or from German/Yiddish, *tago* 'day', *lau* 'according to') – hence its inclusion in this book. However, it also contains words from Slavic (*ludi* 'play', *po* 'at a rate of', *prava* 'correct, right'), and even the odd word from other European languages (from Ancient Greek, *kaj* 'and').

Key numbers:
1 unu, 2 du, 3 tri, 4 kvar, 5 kvin, 6 ses, 7 sep, 8 ok, 9 nau;
10 dek, 11 dek unu, 12 dek du, 16 dek ses, 17 dek sep;
20 dudek, 21 dudek unu; 100 cent; 1000 mil;
456789 kvarcent kvindek ses mil sepcent okdek nau.

Esperanto has an innovative (but at first sight unfamiliar) list of "correlatives", which cover most pronouns and determiners; it also has personal pronouns in a specific class of their own.

Key correlatives:
- *kio* 'what', *kiu* 'which, who', *kia* 'what kind of', *kie* 'where', *kiam* 'when', *kiom* 'how many', *kial* 'why', *kiel* 'how';
- *io* 'something', *ĉiu* 'everyone', *nenia* 'no kind of', *tie* 'there'.

Personal pronouns (1st, 2nd, 3rd person, masculine/feminine/neuter):
- Singular *mi, vi, li/ŝi/ĝi*; plural *ni, vi, ili*; indefinite *oni*.

Object forms add the accusative marker *-n*, and possessives the adjective marker *-a* (thus *ni* 'we', *nin* 'us', *nia* 'our'; *ili* 'they', *ilin* 'them', *ilia* 'their'); the possessive form agrees with the noun (*ili vidis niajn arbarojn* 'they saw our forests').

The indefinite pronoun is widely used to avoid the passive: *oni diras, ke ŝi estos tie* 'it is said [one says] that she will be there'.

Vocabulary is often built up through a series of meaningful affixes – for example *arbo* 'tree' plus *-ar-* 'collection' gives *arbaro* 'forest'. A resultant feature is the creation of opposites through the prefix *mal-*: *rapida* 'fast', *malrapida* 'slow'; *granda* 'big', *malgranda* 'small'.

6.4   Grammar

Peculiarly, word classes are generally marked by endings in Esperanto. Nouns are marked by *-o*; this is amended to *-oj* for the plural. They can also be in the "accusative" case (when used as direct objects of a verb or to mark motion towards), marked by the ending *-n*.

Verbs, which take the ending -*i* as infinitives, are otherwise marked by endings for one of three tenses or two moods but not both ("conditional" is generally regarded as a mood rather than a tense in Esperanto, although this distinction is of no practical relevance). These endings are present -*as*, past -*is*, future -*os*, conditional -*us* and subjunctive/imperative -*u*. Unlike Italic and Germanic languages, tense is relative (i.e. if referring to a future event in the past, the future is used: *mi vidis, ke vi estos tie* 'I saw that you would [will] be there').

Esperanto also allows zero subject in some circumstances (where English typically requires a dummy subject, such as 'it' or 'there'):
- *pluvas multe* 'it is raining a lot';
- *estas tri arboj tie* 'there are three trees there'.

Adjectives are marked by the ending -*a* and agree with their noun, typically appearing after it, although this is stylistic: *arbaro granda* 'a big forest'; *en arbarojn grandajn* 'into big forests'. However, words which by convention always appear before the noun (the article and numbers) do not agree: *en la tri arbarojn grandajn* 'into the three big forests'. Adverbs are marked by the ending -*e*; notably, they tend to be used with the verb 'be' (similarly to Slavic languages, but not Italic or Germanic): *estas klare, ke mi vidis arbaron grandan* 'it is clear that I saw a big forest'.

Although it is not strictly standard usage, in modern Esperanto adjectives and adverbs can be turned directly into verbs in preference to using a construction with *esti* 'be':
- *estas grave, ke vi ne vidis tion / gravas, ke vi ne vidis tion* 'it matters that you did not see that';
- *vi laŭdire estas prava / vi laŭdire pravas* 'apparently you are right';
- *la pilko estas blua / la pilko bluas* 'the ball is blue'.

Exactly when this is deemed permissible varies according to usage and style.

The only article is *la* 'the'. By convention (as there are no actual rules governing its use), it is used as a definite article appearing before the noun. However, there is considerable variation in its usage, and if in doubt it may generally be omitted.

Prepositions, at least in standard usage, have strict meanings which must not be breached.

Key prepositions:
- case prepositions are *de* 'of', *al* 'to', *kun* 'with';
- other prepositions include *por* 'for', *per* 'by', *en* 'in', *ĉe* 'at'.

Prepositions generally do <u>not</u> take the "accusative" form of the noun or pronoun; case prepositions never do: *al iu arbaro* 'to any forest'; *por nia frato* 'for our brother'; *kun ili* 'with them'.

The "accusative" is only used after other (i.e. non-case) prepositions specifically to mark motion towards: *en arbaro* 'in a forest'; *al arbaro* 'to a forest'; *en arbaro<u>n</u>* 'in<u>to</u> a forest'.

There is a spare preposition *je* for when the use of another preposition would be unclear. However, in the modern language, this is often ignored and use of prepositions is increasingly in line with English:
- *je 1887 / en 1887* 'in 1887';
- *je mila fojo / por mila fojo* 'for the thousandth time'.

Word order is typically SVO; but the passive is generally avoided, which can give different word orders (*mi vidis arbaron grandan* 'I saw a big forest'; *arbaron grandan mi vidis* 'a big forest was seen by me').

Yes/no questions require the particle *ĉu:*
- *ŝi kantas* 'she sings'; *ĉu ŝi kantas?* 'does she sing?'

Answer *jes* 'yes'; *ne* 'no'. There is a tendency to reinforce responses: *jes, ĝuste* 'yes, absolutely'.

6.5   Character

Esperanto is deceptively Italic-looking. In fact, its phonology and some of its characteristics (notably the question particle *ĉu*) are markedly Slavic, a product of its geographical origin.

The *Fundamento* (6.2) also provides for the letter *ŭ,* used in practice only in the combination *-aŭ* (another Slavic influence) to specify it is a diphthong and the *a* should not be stressed. This accent mark is now regarded as optional and, for the sake of simplicity, it has been ignored in this chapter.

The language is subject to a notable controversy around its apparent inherent sexism. A significant share of Esperanto's basic vocabulary consists of default masculine words from which feminine forms are then derived: *frato* 'brother', *fratino* 'sister'; *doktoro* '(male) doctor', *doktorino* 'female doctor'. This is the topic of fierce debate among its advocates and critics alike.

Adverbs and word-building are a key feature of Esperanto, particularly when combined: *mia* 'my' + *opinio* 'opinion' = *miaopinie* 'in my opinion'; *plena* 'full, complete' + *Esperanto* = *plenesperante* 'completely in Esperanto'; *kontrau* 'against, opposing' + *flanko* 'side' = *kontrauflanke* 'on the other side, opposite'.

Patro nia, kiu estas en la ĉielo, Via nomo estu sanktigata. Venu Via regno, fariĝu Via volo, kiel en la ĉielo, tiel ankau sur la tero. Nian panon ĉiutagan donu al ni hodiau. Kaj pardonu al ni niajn ŝuldojn, kiel ankau ni pardonas al niaj ŝuldantoj. Kaj ne konduku nin en tenton, sed liberigu nin de la malbono.

7

ITALIAN

Italian, spoken by around 70 million people as a mother tongue and over 100 million in all, is a major European language (also spoken by a significant diaspora elsewhere) but, purely in terms of numbers of speakers, lacks the global reach of many of the other languages discussed in this book. However, those comparatively low numbers belie its true global significance as a language of culture, notably in music and cuisine.

Moreover, for those wishing to acquire a good knowledge of all the languages derived from Latin, Italian may be the best one to start with. This is because its vocabulary is closest to Vulgar Latin, its grammar reflects both French and Spanish (and is thus something of an intermediary between them), and in general it displays some peculiarities typical of Latinate languages without being so structurally complex as to be inaccessible.

7.1   Phonology

It is not for nothing that Italian is regarded as lyrical and romantic. Excepting some common short words, native Italian words must end in a vowel. Italian is also lacking in hard sounds. This is what makes it, in every sense, a musical language.

English speakers are often confused by the <ch> and <gh> spellings, which mark hard consonants /k/ and /g/ respectively before a high vowel (<e> or <i>): *pistacchio, bruschetta* (both with /k/); *spaghetti*. The soft versions are affricates (English <ch>; <j>): *cello; gioia* 'joy'.

Uniquely among major Latin-derived languages, in modern Italian double consonants are so pronounced (*pizza, cappuccino, penne*) and initial consonant clusters with *s-* are now allowed (*scuola* 'school'; *Spagna* 'Spain'). Some consonant clusters have vocalized /l/: *bianco* 'white [blank]'; *chiaro* 'clear'; *fiamma* 'flame'; *piacere* 'pleasure'.

Italian is pronounced forward in the mouth and retains Late Latin's system of all syllables being broadly the same length, with stressed syllables (typically penultimate, but there are numerous exceptions) pronounced with clear emphasis but without notable lengthening.

7.2   Standard

L'Italia è fatta; restano da fare gli italiani 'Now we have created Italy, we must create Italians' goes the famous quote from shortly after the *Risorgimento* (and Italian unification) of the mid 19th century. Even now, Italians generally speak of Italian "languages" (plural), reflecting a wide range of traditional regional dialects descended from Latin.

Nevertheless, the Tuscan of Dante had become the prestige dialect across much of the Italian peninsula even before political unity, and Standard Italian came to be based on it (while still allowing for some significant regional variation). The standard written form thus derives from the literary language of Florence in the early 14th century but, unlike English and French, even the spoken version is based directly on it. Therefore, despite its conservatism (meaning Italian remains the closest national language to Classical Latin in time as well as geography), even modern pronunciation does closely reflect spelling.

Italian rules around written accents allow for some variation, and they are sometimes omitted altogether in informal writing. Grave accents may be used on any vowel to mark stress when it is not on the penultimate syllable (*mèdico* 'doctor'), particularly if it is crucial to mark words apart (*àncora* 'anchor', *ancora* 'still'); however, this is typically insisted upon only if it is a final vowel (*città* 'town, city'). Grave accents may also be used to distinguish words (*è* 'is' versus *e* 'and'); or to mark the strengthened vowel in a diphthong, *più* 'more'.

There is also an acute accent to mark an open <e> (*perché* 'why'); dictionaries mark an open <o> similarly with *ó* but in practice this is seldom encountered in modern writing. The circumflex, once a grammatical marker, has fallen out of use. However, apostrophes where similar vowels run together across words are usually required in all written registers: *sessant'anni* 'sixty years', *dov'è?* 'where is it?', *un bell'uomo* 'a handsome man'.

7.3 Vocabulary

Italian vocabulary is overwhelmingly of Late Latin origin (3.3), with relatively few other influences. There was notable borrowing directly from French around and after the Renaissance, and there is significant recent influence from English.

Key numbers:
1 uno, 2 due, 3 tre, 4 quattro, 5 cinque, 6 sei, 7 sette, 8 otto, 9 nove;
10 dieci, 11 undici, 12 dodici, 15 quindici, 16 sedici, 17 diciassette;
20 venti, 21 ventuno, 26 ventisei; 100 cento; 1000 mille;
456789 quattrocentocinquantaseimilasettecentottantanove.

Italian personal pronouns have shifted markedly in recent centuries. The most noteworthy pronoun is *ci,* which has a wide range of uses including, since late Medieval times, as a first person plural object pronoun 'us' (replacing *nos* as it switched towards *ni,* cf. *vi*).

Personal pronouns (masculine/feminine):

	Singular (1st, 2nd, 3rd)			Plural (1st, 2nd, 3rd)		
Subject	*io*	*tu*	*lui/lei*	*noi*	*voi*	*loro*
Prepositional	*me*	*te*	*lui/lei*	*noi*	*voi*	*loro*
Direct object	*mi*	*ti*	*lo/la*	*ci*	*vi*	*li/le*
Indirect object	*mi*	*ti*	*gli/le*	*ci*	*vi*	*gli*
Possessive	*mio*	*tuo*	*suo*	*nostro*	*vostro*	*loro*

Possessive forms except the third person plural *loro* 'their' agree with their noun in gender and number (*mio-mia-miei-mie; tuo-tua-tuoi-tue; suo-sua-suoi-sue; nostro/-a/-i/-e; vostro/-a/-i/-e*). Notably, possessive pronouns and possessive adjectives are not distinguished in Italian.

Reflexive forms are the same as object forms except the third person (singular and plural) form *si* 'himself/herself/itself/themselves'. Old third person subject pronouns *egli/ella* have fallen out of common use.

Italian exhibits a distinction between familiar and polite forms of 'you'. In the singular, the third person feminine singular form (capitalized; *Lei* etc) doubles as polite 'you', with third person verb forms; however, in the plural, *Voi* is maintained as the polite form (though likewise capitalized in writing): *grazie a Lei* 'Thanks to you [singular]'; *Vi ringrazio per aver guardato* 'I thank you [plural] for having watched'.

The indirect object *gli* becomes *glie* when combined with another object pronoun: *glielo do* 'I give it to him'. Similarly, *mi/ti/ci/vi* become *me/te/ce/ve* when so combined: *ce lo danno* 'They give it to us'.

Ci is also used effectively as a dummy subject (*ci sono* tre mele qui 'there are three apples here') and as a locative pronoun (*ce l'avevo vista* 'I had seen her there'), making it extremely widespread. There is also a specific genitive pronoun *ne* (*ne* avete tre 'you have three of them').

Demonstrative pronouns are *questo/-a/-i/-e* 'this, these', *quello/-a/-i/-e* 'that, those': *questo cielo* 'this sky', *quelle mele* 'those apples'.

Interrogative/Relative pronouns include *chi* 'who', *che* 'what', *dove* 'where', *quando* 'when', *come* 'how', *(il/la/i/le) quale/-i* 'which', *quanto/-a/-i/-e* 'how much/many', and prepositional form *cui* (*di cui* 'of which, whose'); *ciò* is used as a relative pronoun of general reference (*tutto ciò che ho* 'all [of what] I have').

The word *cosa* 'thing' is often used as an interrogative pronoun in the modern language: *cos'è?* 'what is it?'; *tu cosa vedi?* 'what do you see?'

7.4   Grammar

Italian nouns are one of two genders, marked singular or plural. Masculine nouns often end singular *-o*, plural *-i*; feminine singular *-a*, plural *-e*; with another set of either gender (though the common endings *-ione* and *-udine* are always feminine) ending singular *-e*, plural *-i*.

There are some irregular plurals (e.g. *uomo-uomini* 'man-men'); there is also some variation around what happens to preceding vowels (e.g. *arancia-arance* 'orange-oranges' but *valigia-valigie* 'case-cases') or if the last consonant is <c> or <g> (e.g. masculine *amico-amici* but feminine *amica-amiche* 'friend-friends').

Verb endings of *cantare* 'sing', (-*a*- stem; 1st, 2nd, 3rd person).

Present indicative ('sing'):
- singular *canto, canti, canta;*
- plural *cantiamo, cantate, cantano.*

Present subjunctive:
- singular *canti, canti, canti;*
- plural *cantiamo, cantiate, cantino.*

Imperfect indicative ('used to sing'):
- singular *cantavo, cantavi, cantava;*
- plural *cantavamo, cantavate, cantavano.*

Imperfect subjunctive:
- singular *cantassi, cantassi, cantasse;*
- plural *cantassimo, cantaste, cantassero.*

Future ('will sing'):
- singular *canterò, canterai, canterà;*
- plural *canteremo, canterete, canteranno.*

Conditional ('would sing'):
- singular *canterei, canteresti, canterebbe;*
- plural *canteremmo, cantereste, canterebbero.*

Imperatives are singular *canta* (polite *canti*), plural *cantate*; participles are past *cantato*, present *cantando*. Past participles are often irregular in Italian and may be best learned alongside each verb. Before a participle or another infinitive, the infinitive loses final -*e*: *aver guardato* 'to have watched'; *poter vedere* 'to be able to see'.

Italian is a pro-drop language, meaning verbs can be used without the subject if the subject is clear: *amo* 'I love', *finiscono* 'they finish', *l'abbiamo visto* 'we saw it'.

Most verbs fall into four conjugations, easily identified by their infinitive endings which are aligned directly with Latin (stressed *-are,* stressed *-ere,* unstressed *-ere* and stressed *-ire*); there are also some common irregulars. They are marked for tense (and aspect) and agree with their subject noun; both indicative and subjunctive moods are in widespread use even in the modern spoken language. Indicative endings may mark present, imperfect, conditional or future tenses (also past in the written language); combinations with the verb *avere* 'have' or *essere* 'be', the latter of which requires subject-participle agreement, may also mark perfect (or general past tense in speech), pluperfect or future perfect (*ho creduto* 'I have believed'; *eravamo andati* 'we had gone'; *avranno visto* 'they will have seen'). Near future can be marked with *andare a* 'go to' plus infinitive (*vado a cantare* 'I am off to sing'); *stare* 'be, stand' is used for immediate future with *per* plus infinitive (*sto per cantare* 'I am about to sing'), or for progressive aspect plus present participle (*sto cantando* 'I am singing'; *stavano finendo* 'they were finishing'; no participle agreement). Fewer tense endings are in use with the subjunctive, although the full range of tenses and aspects using the subjunctive forms of auxiliaries *avere, essere, andare* and *stare* is available. The passive is typically formed with *essere* or *venire* 'come' plus past participle and preposition *da* (*è stato costruito qui dai Romani* 'it was built here by the Romans'), although a reflexive may often be preferred with this meaning (*si scrivono nello stesso modo* 'they are written [they write themselves] in the same way').

Comparison in Italian uses *più* or *meno* usually accompanied by *di* (*ne ho meno di lei* 'I have fewer than her'; *ne ho più di due* 'I have more than two'); *che* replaces *di* if a new clause or adjective follows (*era più che sufficiente* 'it was more than sufficient'). Equative for quantities is via *tanto... quanto* 'as many... as' or otherwise *così ... come* 'as ... as'; here, the initial word (*tanto* or *così*) is often omitted.

Adjectives agree in number and gender with their noun in all circumstances, based on the same set of endings (singular *-o/-a*, plural *-i/-e*; or singular *-e*, plural *-i*). Attributively, they tend to go after the noun (particularly if stating a fact, like nationality or colour: *le valigie rosse* 'the red suitcases'; *un giardino inglese* 'an English garden'), but adjectives of general description or opinion may precede (*un piccolo uomo* 'a little man'; *la dolce vita* 'the sweet life'). Adverbs are commonly formed by adding the ending *-mente* to the feminine form of the adjective (*vero* 'true', *veramente* 'truly, really'); there are common irregular forms (*bene* 'well'; *male* 'badly').

Articles:

	Definite		Indefinite	
	Masculine	Feminine	Masculine	Feminine
Singular	*il, lo (l')*	*la (l')*	*i, gli*	*le*
Plural	*un, uno*	*una (un')*	*dei, degli*	*delle*

Definite articles are commonly used with reference to abstract terms, languages and countries (*l'Italia è fatta* 'Italy is made') but are often omitted after prepositions in set phrases (*in_cucina* 'in the kitchen'). Partitive articles with *di* are frequent, particularly in the north, though not compulsory (*vorrei del burro* 'I would like some butter'). The masculine definite articles become *lo/gli* before vowels and certain consonant clusters (*lo zucchero* 'the sugar'; *gli scudetti* 'the shields'; *gli uomini* 'the men'); elided forms are usual in writing before vowels in the singular (*l'uomo* 'the man'; *l'emulsione* 'the emulsion') but are not used in the plural (*le emulsioni* 'the emulsions').

When used as adjectives, possessive forms are almost always combined with the definite article: *la mia borsa* 'my bag'; *il nostro scudetto* 'our shield'. One notable exception is with singular family members: *mia sorella* 'my sister' (but *le mie sorelle* 'my sisters').

Prepositions take full prepositional (object) pronouns: *con te* 'with you'; *a noi* 'to us'. There is one adverb derived from a verb which now behaves as a lone postposition, curiously exactly as in English (but not any other major Latin-derived language): *due anni fa* 'two years ago'.

Key prepositions:
- *di* 'of', *a* 'to, at', *in* 'in', *da* 'from', *con* 'with', *per* 'by, for'.

Some combine with the definite article, often with modifications: (*di+lo=dello; a+la=alla, in+gli=negli, da+il=dal* etc).

Word order is typically SVO (SOV if the object is a pronoun), but verb first is frequent particularly in subordinate clauses: *lo zucchero che ha visto mia sorella* 'the sugar (that) my sister saw'. When forming the perfect, participles may agree with a direct object appearing before them, but typically this applies only if it is a third person pronoun: *le canzoni che hanno scritto* (rarely *scritte*) 'the songs they wrote'; *l'ho visto* 'I saw <u>him</u>'; *l'ho vista* 'I saw her'. Negation is via the simple particle *non,* placed before the verb and any object pronouns (*non c'è del burro* 'there is no butter'); this may be combined with negative adverbs typically appearing after the verb (*niente* 'nothing', *nulla* 'none') or with common adverbs *mica* 'hardly' or *mai* 'ever' which then take on a negative meaning (*non lo vedi mai* 'you <u>never</u> see it').

Yes/no questions rely merely on intonation:
* *canta* 'she sings'; *canta?* 'does she sing?'

Answer *sì* 'yes'; *no* 'no'.

7.5 Character

Modern Italian is literally a very musical language, for which it is well suited given the predominance of vowels and soft sounds.

However, Italian does have a perhaps surprising preference for nouns combined with a relatively small number of key verbs, most notably *fare* 'do, make' (*ho fatto un'investigazione del caso* 'I investigated the case [I did an investigation of the case]'). *Fare* in fact covers a remarkable range of meanings: *fare una doccia* 'take a shower'; *fare una domanda* 'ask a question'; *fare la professora* 'be a teacher'; *fare sport* 'play sport'; *fare colazione* 'eat breakfast'; *fare la spesa* 'go shopping'; *fare la valigia* 'pack a suitcase'.

Padre nostro, che sei nei cieli, sia santificato il tuo nome; venga il tuo regno; sia fatta la tua voluntà, come in cielo, così in terra. Dacci oggi il nostro pane quotidiano e rimetti a noi i nostri debiti, come noi li rimettiamo ai nostri debitori, e non ci indurre in tentazione, ma liberaci dal male.

8

PORTUGUESE

Even though it is sometimes overlooked because of its proximity (both geographical and linguistic) to Spanish, Portuguese has become a significant global language given its predominance in Brazil. It was also the first Indo-European language to spread to sub-Saharan Africa, and it holds the curious distinction of being currently the most widely spoken language in the Southern Hemisphere.

Portuguese is split into two distinct varieties: *português brasileiro* 'Brazilian Portuguese', as spoken in Brazil; and *português continental* 'Continental Portuguese', often referred to as "European" Portuguese in English but retaining its direct translation here to emphasize that it is also the variety upon which Portuguese in Africa is largely based.

8.1   Phonology

In the late first millennium, what became Portuguese was already characterized by the retention of the vowel structure of Vulgar Latin but the loss of key consonants. Continental Portuguese in particular is easily distinguished by how clipped the remaining vowels can sound, notably between consonants and at the end of words (final <e> is generally barely pronounced in rapid speech, particularly in Portugal).

One of many outcomes of this phonological development was a distinctive nasalization, marked variously in writing (*nação* 'nation', *portagem* 'toll gate', *muito* 'very, much').

Portuguese is further characterized by its slushy sound. In most varieties, particularly in Brazil, <d> and <t> are somewhat palatalized before <i> or unstressed <e>, thus sounding close to English <j> (*cidade* 'city'; *dia* 'day'; *antigamente* 'formerly'). There is also a reduction of a series of initial consonant clusters ending in /l/ in Latin, usually to a sibilant written and pronounced similarly to English <ch> (*chover* 'rain' < Vulgar Latin *plovere*; *chama* 'flame' < *flamma*; *chave* 'key' < *clavis*); in some cases these have simply shifted /l/ to /r/ (*branco* 'white [blank]'; *prazer* 'pleasure'). Final -*l* after a vowel is also semi-vocalized in Brazil, pronounced close to /w/ (*mal* 'badly'). Continental Portuguese and some urban Brazilian dialects are also marked for their pronunciation of <s>, which before a consonant or at the end of a word sounds close to English <sh> (*nações* 'nations', *escola* 'school').

In all varieties, <s> (or <x>) may be voiced or voiceless depending on environment (*mesmas* 'same [feminine plural]'); <r> is always trilled, close to English <h> in most contexts or soft <d> in others; these may be doubled in writing for etymological reasons, but are treated as single in speech (*passar* 'pass', *barriga* 'belly'); <x> is palatalized (close to English <sh>), notably after diphthongs (*peixe* 'fish'). Palatized /l/ and /n/ are written with a following <h> (*filho* 'son'; *Espanha* 'Spain'). The open or closed nature of vowels is sometimes marked by written accents (8.2), but not always as it can also vary depending on dialect.

Brazilian and Continental Portuguese are easily distinguishable from each other. The latter is notable for being "stress-timed", meaning stressed syllables are particularly prominent in speech (in this sense it is more similar to Germanic languages); in terms of stress and general rhythm, Brazilian varieties are markedly closer to Spanish and Italian.

What in English is known as a "tilde" (e.g. ã, õ), now a full accent mark in Portuguese and Spanish, was originally a following *n* marked by calligraphers above the previous letter to save space.

8.2   Standard

Portuguese has a bizarre history well beyond the scope of this chapter, not least because its first identifiable form came not in modern Portugal at all, but in the now Spanish region of Galicia to the north. Essentially, three major modern Latin-derived languages spread south during the *Reconquista* of the Iberian Peninsula – Catalan to the east, Castilian Spanish in the middle and Galician to the west. Those Galician speakers heading south ended up founding the Kingdom of Portugal (while those who remained in Galicia ended up in Spain).

The standardization of Portuguese, begun when it was recognized as the common language of the people in the late 13th century (at the same time as the foundation of the first university in Portugal, now in Coimbra), was complex. The emergence of literary norms struggled to deal with a significant sound shift in the late Middle Ages. The practical outcome is that the language has far more variations in vowels than neighbouring Castilian Spanish, thus requiring a much wider range of accent marks – alongside the cedilla *ç* to soften <c> before a low vowel (*praça* 'square') and the tilde (8.1) to mark nasalization (*mão* 'hand'), there are acutes and circumflexes to mark open and closed stressed vowels respectively (*avó* 'grandmother' but *avô* 'grandfather') and graves to mark consecutive same letters grammatically, now usually only affecting <a> (*à* 'to the [feminine singular]').

Galician remains a regional language of Spain with its own disputes around standardization. It is now linguistically somewhere between Standard Castilian Spanish and Standard Portuguese.

Unusually among major European languages, spelling standardization was largely carried out by one man, Gonçalves Viana, tasked to carry it out at the beginning of the Portuguese Republic shortly before the Great War. Passing this task to one man, and assuming that the main aim was direct phonemic representation, caused its own problems, again beyond the scope of this chapter. Perhaps Portuguese spelling is best described as complex, but it is also undeniably consistent. (Brazil adopted its own similar but not identical Standard some decades later.)

Although such things are difficult to quantify exactly, the differences between Brazilian and Continental Portuguese are probably greater than between, for example, American and British English. Not only do some spellings and items of vocabulary vary, but the grammar is markedly different. By most accounts, Portuguese speakers elsewhere in the world have little difficulty understanding Brazilians (given the widespread availability of Brazilian media) but, particularly when speech becomes more informal and colloquial, the reverse is not always true. A controversial *Acordo Ortográfico* 'orthographical agreement' on spelling reform in the late 20th century sought to bring the varieties of Portuguese closer together. However, this was ignored to such an extent that many dictionaries now contain both *antes do Acordo* 'pre-agreement' and *depois do Acordo* 'post-agreement' spellings, and many prominent writers and translators specify that they have rejected the agreement.

8.3   Vocabulary

Portuguese vocabulary is largely of Early Latin origin (2.3), though Portugal's history under Arabic-speaking rule and subsequently as an imperial power itself have led to some other influences.

Key numbers:
1 um, 2 dois/duas, 3 três, 4 quatro, 5 cinco, 6 seis, 7 sete, 8 oito, 9 nove;
10 dez, 11 onze, 12 doze, 15 quinze, 16 dezesseis, 17 dezessete;
20 vinte, 21 vinte e um; 100 cem (cento); 1000 mil;
456789 quatrocentos e cinquenta e seis mil setecentos e oitenta e nove.

Meia is preferred to *seis* 'six' in lists (e.g. phone numbers).

High teen numbers are written *dezasseis, dezassete* etc in Continental Portuguese.

A key word in Portuguese without obvious parallel is *ficar* 'be, get, end up' – notably broader meanings than its cognates in other languages.

Personal pronouns (masculine/feminine):

	Singular (1st, 2nd, 3rd)			Plural (1st, 2nd, 3rd)		
Subject	*eu*	*tu, você*	*ele/ela*	*nós*	*vocês*	*eles/elas*
Prepositional	*mim*	*ti, você*				
Object	*me*	*te, lhe*	*o/a; lhe*	*nos*	*lhes*	*os/as; lhes*

Reflexive forms are the same as object forms except third person *se* (both genders; *se* is also therefore the reflexive form for *você/vocês*).

As in Spanish (discussed at 9.3), there are peculiar prepositional forms with *com* 'with': *comigo* 'with me', *contigo* 'with you', *consigo* 'with you/himself/herself/itself/themselves', *conosco* 'with us'.

Você(s), which typically takes a third person verb form, is the normal polite form of address. In most varieties *vocês* has taken over completely from the archaic *vós* (object *vos*) in the plural; in the singular usage varies, with *você* preferred to *tu/te* in much but not all of Brazil; *tu/te* is still in regular use in Continental Portuguese.

The third person forms *o* and *a* (also *os/as*) are used as direct objects, with *lhe(s)* indirect; however, when attached to the verb they cause changes: generally, the final consonant of the verb is removed and replaced by *l* (*diz+o=dilo* 'say it'); but with final nasal consonants *n* is added (*tem+as=temnas* 'have them'). In Continental Portuguese, contractions are also applied to object pronouns appearing together: *eu dou-lho* 'I give it to him/her'. This is all tied to a system of clitics unique among major Latin-derived languages which even allows the pronoun to be placed between the verb stem and the ending. The result of all of this can confuse even native speakers, and in practice usage also varies significantly between Brazilian and Continental Portuguese.

Portuguese also makes widespread use of *a gente* 'the people' as a pronoun, equivalent to English 'one'; this should be followed by a third person singular verb. Similarly, *o senhor* 'the gentleman' or *a senhora* 'the lady' (or equivalent plurals) may be used as a highly formal form of address.

Possessive pronouns agree with their noun; they are (masculine/feminine; 1st, 2nd, 3rd person):
- singular *meu(s)/minha(s), teu(s)/tua(s), seu(s)/sua(s);*
- plural *nosso(s)/nossa(s), vosso(s)/vossa(s), seu(s)/sua(s).*

Seu/sua is also used with *vocês* (so *vosso* is very rarely encountered); however, to avoid confusion, *de* plus pronoun is often preferred: *de você(s)* 'your', *dele* 'his, its [masc.]', *delas* 'their [fem.]', etc (8.4).

Demonstrative pronouns exhibit three grades: *este/esta(s)* 'this (these)'; *esse/essa(s)* 'that (those)'; *aquele/aquela(s)* 'that (those) yonder'; "neuter" singular forms for general use also occur: *isto; isso; aquilo*. Interrogative and relative pronouns are largely the same as each other: *quem* 'who', *(o) que* 'what, that', *quando* 'when', *onde* 'where', *como* how', *(o/a) qual, (os/as) quais* 'which': *o que é isto* 'what is this?'

8.4   Grammar

Portuguese nouns have one of two genders, masculine often ending *-o* and feminine often ending *-a* (but *-ão* is typically feminine). Plural generally adds *-(e)s*, but with exceptions (including *-ão* to *-ões*; *-em* to *-ens*; *-l* to *-is*: *nações* 'nations', *portagens* 'toll gates', *hotéis* 'hotels').

Verb endings of *cantar* 'sing',
(*-a-* stem; 1st, 2nd, 3rd person singular; 1st, 3rd person plural).

Present indicative ('sing'):
- *canto, cantas, canta; cantamos, cantam.*

Present subjunctive:
- *cante, cantes, cante; cantemos, cantem.*

Imperfect indicative ('used to sing'):
- *cantava, cantavas, cantava; cantávamos, cantavam.*

Imperfect subjunctive:
- *cantasse, cantasses, cantasse; cantássemos, cantassem.*

Preterite ('sang'):
- *cantei, cantaste, cantou; cantamos, cantaram.*

Pluperfect ('had sung'):
- *cantara, cantaras, cantara; cantáramos, cantaram.*

Future indicative ('will sing'):
- *cantarei, cantarás, cantará; cantaremos, cantarão.*

Future subjunctive:
- *cantar, cantares, cantar; cantarmos, cantarem.*

Conditional ('would sing'):
- *cantaria, cantarias, cantaria; cantaríamos, cantariam.*

Imperative ('sing!'):
- singular *canta* (polite *cante); plural *cantem.*

Second person verb forms, even in the singular, are rare in Brazil (generally replaced by third person forms even in areas where *tu/te* are still in use as second person pronouns).

There are also participles (past *cantado,* present *cantando*), as well as a series of personal infinitives which typically take the same form as the future subjunctive. The future subjunctive was absent even in Classical Latin (2.4), and so it is an innovation in Iberian languages which has been fully retained even in colloquial spoken Portuguese.

The Portuguese verb, which is split into three regular conjugations ending -*ar,* -*er* and -*ir* alongside many common irregulars, is extraordinarily complex. Not only are there endings in regular use to mark present, past preterite, past imperfect, future and conditional, but also the pluperfect; it also has a full range of past, present and future subjunctive endings. Portuguese exceptionally uses *ter* 'have, hold' (cf. Spanish *haber*) as the auxiliary verb to form the perfect (*eles têm cantado* 'they have sung'). The verb *ir* 'go' plus infinitive can be used for immediate future (*eu vou cantar* 'I am going to sing'). As in Spanish there are two verbs translated in English by 'be', *estar* and *ser,* and both have auxiliary uses. *Estar* is used to form the progressive, with the present participle in Brazilian or *a* plus infinitive in Continental (*eles estão fazendo / estão a fazer* 'they are doing'). *Ser* is generally used with the past participle and the preposition *por* to form the passive (*foi construído aqui pelos romanos* 'it was built here by the Romans'), although reflexive constructions are also possible (*Português se fala em Moçambique* 'Portuguese is spoken in Mozambique').

Portuguese is a pro-drop language, meaning verbs can be used without the subject if the subject is clear: *canto* 'I sing'; *terminam* 'they finish'; *o vimos* 'we saw it'. However, in the 21st century, unlike in other Latinate languages, there is a marked tendency towards including the subject regardless, particularly in Brazil: *eu canto; eles terminam; nós o vimos.*

Portuguese adjectives agree with nouns in all positions; generally, they appear after them attributively: *a língua inglesa* 'the English language'.

Articles:

	Definite		Indefinite	
	Masculine	Feminine	Masculine	Feminine
Singular	*o*	*a*	*um*	*uma*
Plural	*os*	*as*	*uns*	*umas*

The forms of Portuguese articles are exceptional. The definite has been reduced, and typically appears before possessives (*a minha chave* 'my key'). The indefinite article has a distinct plural, which as in Spanish is used typically to mean 'some, a number of' (*umas chaves* 'a number of keys'). Uniquely among major Latin-derived languages, the article is almost always used with countries and regions in all contexts (*no Brasil* 'in Brazil', *da França* 'from France', *ao Algarve* 'to the Algarve'); *Portugal, Angola* and *Moçambique* are among notable exceptions (*em Portugal* 'in Portugal', *de Angola* 'from Angola').

Common prepositions:
- *de* 'of, from', *a* 'to, at', *por* 'for, by', *para* 'for, towards', *com* 'with', *em* 'in' (but reduced to *n-* when combined, see below).

Most of these are combined with articles, adverbs of place, pronouns and demonstratives as a single word where they run together, sometimes with further modifications:
- *da* 'of the' [feminine sg.], *ao* 'to the' [masculine sg.], *às* 'to the' [feminine pl.], *pelos* 'for the' [masculine pl.], *no* 'in the' [masculine sg.], *numa* 'in a' [feminine sg.];
- *daqui* 'from here'; *dela* '(of) it, her', *neles* 'in them [masc.]';
- *neste* 'in this'; *dessas* 'from those'; *àquela* 'at that (yonder)'.

Word order is typically SVO, or SOV where the object is a personal pronoun. However, the exact order of items where personal pronouns appear as objects is complex (and varies also between Brazilian and Continental usage; 8.3). Negation is relatively straightforward, with the particle *não* placed before the verb and sometimes accompanied by a negative pronoun after (most commonly *nada* 'nothing' or *nunca* 'never'): *não vimos nada* 'we did not see anything / we saw nothing' (i.e. negative words reinforce rather than cancel out).

Yes/no questions rely on intonation or rephrase with *é que* 'is it that':
- *ela canta* 'she sings';
- *ela canta? / é que ela canta?* 'does she sing?'

Answer *sim* 'yes'; *não* 'no'; speakers may repeat the verb to emphasize an affirmative: *(sim,) canta* 'yes, she sings'.

8.5   Character

Portuguese is a rhythmically markedly different language from Spanish or Italian; while structurally similar particularly to Spanish, it sounds clearly distinct.

One noteworthy peculiarity of Portuguese is its naming conventions concerning days of the week. Although the days of the weekend retain their names cognate with other related languages (*sábado* 'Saturday'; *domingo* 'Sunday'), the traditional names of weekdays based on deities found in all other major Germanic and Latinate languages have been abandoned, and replaced simply with ordinal numbers: *segunda-feira* 'Monday' [literally 'second fair day'], *terça-feira* 'Tuesday', *sexta-feira* 'Friday', etc (*feira* is now often dropped in speech). Originally, these names applied specifically to Holy Week, but gradually came to be adopted for any week.

Like Spanish, Portuguese is a notably verb-focused language, with a wide range of subtleties in tense and mood expressed through the huge selection of endings (and combinations of auxiliary verbs) available.

Pai nosso, que estás no céu; santificado seja o teu nome; venha o teu reino; seja feita a tua vontade; assim na terra como no céu; o pão nosso de cada dia nos dai hoje; e perdoai as nossas dívidas; assim como nós perdoamos os nossos devedores; e não nos deixes cair em tentação; mas livrai-nos do mal.

9

SPANISH

Around half a billion people now speak Castilian Spanish natively –
more than any other language in the West and more than all the other
Latin-derived languages combined. That alone makes it a prime
candidate for "most useful language to learn" status.

The name of the language is disputed by speakers themselves.
Castellano 'Castilian' is preferred by some to distinguish it clearly
from other "Spanish languages", such as Catalan, Basque or
Galician; others prefer to emphasize the unitary nature of the country
or of the Spanish-speaking world generally by using *Español*
'Spanish'. The latter is more commonly used by non-speakers, and
for that reason alone (without political or constitutional prejudice) it
is preferred in this book.

Having grown as the administrative language of what was at the time
the greatest Empire the West had ever known, Spanish then expanded
its reach particularly in the Western Hemisphere to its contemporary
position, covering almost the entirety of Central and South America
except Brazil and some of its northern neighbours. This also has the
practical effect of making Spanish an increasingly conspicuous and
influential language in cultural and economic life within the United
States, where it is now spoken by more people than in any other country
except Mexico. It can also serve as a gateway to other Latin-derived
languages, most obviously Portuguese and Italian.

There is a tendency to distinguish between "Peninsular" or "European" Spanish on one hand and "Latin American" Spanish on the other. This distinction has historical merit, but it is somewhat artificial in practice – there is notable variation across the Spanish-speaking world (with varieties spoken in the "Southern Cone" of Argentina, Chile, Paraguay and Uruguay being outstandingly distinct in intonation and aspects of grammar) and even within individual countries. Therefore, the division is nothing like as straightforward as that between American and British English or even between Brazilian and Continental Portuguese (8.2).

Spanish is almost universally now the first or second foreign language taught in schools in Anglophone countries.

9.1 Phonology

Having for many centuries sounded almost identical to Portuguese, Old Spanish underwent a dramatic consonantal sound shift in the late 16th century affecting its sibilants (often written <s> or <z> in English):
- the shift was caused by a simplification of clusters with dental consonants (/dz/ to /z/ and /ts/ to /s/) over the previous century;
- the "hissing" sibilant /ʃ/ (similar to English <sh>), represented by <x> in Old Spanish and modern Portuguese, was then generally retracted to /x/ (i.e. pronounced as Scottish 'lo<u>ch</u>');
- /z/ (now typically written <c> or <z>) was devoiced; and
- the resultant devoiced sound was then drawn forward in most dialects to /θ/ (similar to English <th>), but it merged instead with /s/ in some southern and insular dialects (the ones on which Latin American varieties came to be based).

Silent initial *h-* is now written etymologically in modern Spanish (e.g. *haber* 'have' from Latin *habēre*; this was typically *aver* in Old Spanish, cf. Italian *avere*). As initial *f-* had already shifted to *h-* in most common words (perhaps due to Basque influence), this effectively means initial *f-* has often become silent over time (e.g. *hijo* 'son', *hierro* 'iron'; cf. Portuguese *filho, ferro*; Italian *figlio, ferro*); however, this shift has not applied to less common words (e.g. *ferrocarril* 'rail [iron track]') or to compound words (*<u>h</u>acer* 'do' but *satis<u>f</u>acer* 'satisfy').

Spanish speech has merged <v> and <b>, typically also written etymologically in the modern language. Like Portuguese but unlike Italian, it has also tended towards removing consonants between vowels as well as unstressed vowels between consonants (*ver* 'see', *pueblo* 'people'; cf. Latin *vidēre, pōpulus*; Italian *vedere, popolo*).

As in Portuguese (8.1), <s> may be voiced or voiceless depending on environment (*mismas* 'same [feminine plural]'; first <s> voiced); <r> is slightly trilled, although more so at the start of a word or when doubled in writing (*real* 'royal'; *perro* 'dog'). The conspicuous <ñ> (discussed at 9.2) and <ll> are considered distinct letters in their own right; the latter has merged in some (but not all) varieties with <y> in speech, and has developed widely varying pronunciations across the Spanish-speaking world, ranging from close to English <y> to close to English <j> (the latter is characteristic of Argentina and Uruguay).

With all those developments with consonants, Spanish vowels have also developed to become remarkably simplified, with just five distinct vowel sounds. However, in certain stressed positions two are consistently diphthongized (<e> to <ie> and <o> to <ue>).

As in Italian, but perhaps not quite as obviously, the location of articulation tends to be towards the front of the mouth. Stressed syllables are clearly strengthened (i.e. louder) but not markedly lengthened.

9.2   Standard

Spanish has an Academy, whose most notable and widely accepted intervention was to re-spell the language to reflect modern pronunciation in the early 19th century, while allowing for some etymological distinction (9.1; which also had the effect of catering for some dialect variation) and including inverted punctuation (*¿?* and *¡!*). Therefore, the writing system is considerably more representative of modern daily speech than is the case for languages such as English and French, while also less complex than Portuguese or Italian.

Unlike Brazilian versus Continental Portuguese or American versus British English, there are no significant variations in spellings in the standard language across the Spanish-speaking world. Differences are largely confined to items of vocabulary and some points of grammatical detail, such as choice of past tense or preferred past participle forms.

Although dialects across the Spanish-speaking world are clearly distinguishable, there does exist a "neutral Latin American Spanish" often used in television (e.g. for dubbing). This is designed to combine the most common vocabulary and pronunciation.

Most words in Spanish end in a vowel, *-n* or *-s*. Where this is the case, stress is typically applied on the penultimate syllable; otherwise it is on the final syllable; exceptions require the stress to be marked with an acute accent on the vowel (*plátano* 'banana'; *fácil* 'easy'; *nación* 'nation'). This accent is also used to mark separately pronounced vowels (*día* 'day') or distinction between words (*si* 'if', *sí* 'yes'; see also pronouns, 9.3). The only other written accents are what is known in English as the tilde <ñ> (8.3), formerly a double consonant <nn> but now marking palatization (pronounced as if <ny>, a sound typically written <gn> in French and Italian); and the diaresis <ü> used to mark sounding after hard <g> (thus *vergüenza* 'disgrace', but *guerra* 'war').

9.3   Vocabulary

Spanish vocabulary is overwhelmingly derived from Early Latin (2.3). There was some subsequent influence from the Visigoths (and thus Gothic; 4.5). In later centuries Spain's history both as colonized (predominantly by Arabic speakers, hence *arroz* 'rice', *alcalde* 'mayor', etc) and then colonizer (predominantly in the Americas, hence *chocolate, llama,* etc) means it also draws widely from elsewhere.

Key numbers:
1 uno, 2 dos, 3 tres, 4 cuatro, 5 cinco, 6 seis, 7 siete, 8 ocho, 9 nueve;
10 diez, 11 once, 12 doce, 15 quince, 16 dieciséis, 17 diecisiete;
20 veinte, 21 veintiuno; 100 cien (ciento); 1000 mil;
456789 cuatrocientos cincuenta y seis mil setecientos ochenta y nueve.

Unlike its cognates in Italian, French and even Old Spanish, Modern Spanish restricts *haber* solely to auxiliary use (conversely *tener* 'have' acts predominantly as a main verb); for existential clauses there is a specific present tense form *hay* 'there is, there are'.

Personal pronouns (masculine/feminine):

	Singular (1st, 2nd, 3rd)			Plural (1st, 2nd, 3rd)		
Subject	*yo*	*tú [vos]*	*él/ella*	*nosotros*	*vosotros*	*ellos/ ellas*
Prepositional	*mí*	*ti [vos]*				
Object	*me*	*te*	*lo/la*	*nos*	*os*	*los/las*
(indirect)			*(le)*			*(les)*

Reflexive forms are the same as object forms except third person *se* (both genders, prepositional form *sí*). *Le/les* are described as indirect object pronouns in prescriptive grammars, although usage can vary; they are replaced by *se* if appearing together with another pronoun: *se lo doy* 'I give it to him/her/them' (to specify which, *a él, a ella* or *a ellos/ellas* may be added: *se lo doy a ella* 'I give it to <u>her</u>').

As in Portuguese, the prepositional forms *conmigo* 'with me', *contigo* 'with you', *consigo* 'with himself/herself/itself/themselves' display the *-go* ending. This is derived from the Latin postposition *cum* (3.3), which itself developed subsequently into the preposition *con* 'with'; etymologically, therefore, *con* and *-go* are the same word.

The polite form of address is generally *usted,* plural *ustedes*; this takes a third person verb and object pronoun. The distinction between *tú/vosotros* and *usted(es)* varies between dialects and is only fully observed in Spain itself. In many regions (notably much of Bolivia, Ecuador, Colombia and Venezuela) *vosotros* is abandoned altogether in the plural but the *tú/usted* distinction generally remains in the singular. In parts of Colombia *su merced* (or *sumercé*) may substitute as the polite form, but this is largely unknown elsewhere.

Vos as a second person pronoun is found in parts of numerous countries in Latin America, but it has wholly replaced *tú/ti* in the standard language only in Argentina, Uruguay and Paraguay.

Possessives (masculine/feminine; for plural agreement add -*s*):

	Singular (1st, 2nd, 3rd)			Plural (1st, 2nd, 3rd)		
Adjective	*mi*	*tu*	*su*	*nostro/a*	*vostro/a*	*su*
Pronoun	*mío/a*	*tuyo/a*	*suyo/a*			*suyo/a*

Demonstratives exhibit three degrees of gradation. Determiners are (masculine/feminine): *este/esta(s)* 'this (these)'; *ese/esa(s)* 'that (those)'; *aquel/aquela(s)* 'that (those) yonder'. As pronouns, these should be written with an accent on the *é*; a neuter exists for general reference: *ésto ya no es divertido* 'this is not funny any more'.

Interrogative and relative pronouns are the same as each other, but interrogatives add an accent in writing: *sabes donde está nuestro amigo* 'you know where our friend is'; *¿sabes dónde está nuestro amigo?* 'do you know where our friend is?' This also applies to *quien(es)* 'who', *que* 'what/that', *cuando* 'when', *como* 'how', *cuanto(s)* 'how many/much', *cual(es)* 'which' and prepositional form *cuyo* 'whose': *¿cuál es tu color?* 'which is your colour?'

9.4   Grammar

The Spanish noun, in common with nearly all other Latin-derived languages, is either masculine (typically ending -*o*) or feminine (typically ending -*a*). The plural form is almost always -*(e)s* (with very few exceptions, typically direct borrowings from English or Latin). A notable feature of Spanish is the "interpersonal *a*", whose origins and purpose remain a mystery to linguists; the preposition *a* is required before all animate grammatical objects: *el agua ayuda a mi hijo* 'the water helps my son'; *vimos a Conchita* 'we saw Conchita'.

Verb endings of *cantar* 'sing', (-*a*- stem; 1st, 2nd, 3rd person).

Present indicative ('sing'):
- singular *canto, (tú) cantas* or *(vós) cantás, canta;*
- plural *cantamos, cantáis, cantan.*

Present subjunctive:
- singular *cante, cantes, cante;*
- plural *cantemos, cantéis, canten.*

Imperfect indicative ('used to sing'):
- singular *cantaba, cantabas, cantaba;*
- plural *cantábamos, cantabais, cantaban.*

Imperfect subjunctive:
- sg. *cantara/cantase, cantaras/cantases, cantara/cantase;*
- pl. *cantáramos/cantásemos, cantarais/-seis, cantaran/-sen.*

Preterite ('sang'):
- singular *canté, cantaste, cantó;*
- plural *cantamos, cantasteis, cantaron.*

Future ('will sing'):
- singular *cantaré, cantarás, cantará;*
- plural *cantaremos, cantaréis, cantarán.*

Conditional ('would sing'):
- singular *cantaría, cantarías, cantaría;*
- plural *cantaríamos, cantaríais, cantarían.*

The participles are past *cantado*, present *cantando*; imperatives are singular *canta* (polite *cante*), plural *cantad* (polite *canten*).

The verb is not quite as complex as in Portuguese (8.4), but separate past preterite and imperfect endings do run alongside present, future and conditional; there is also a present subjunctive form as well as, curiously, two more or less interchangeable past subjunctive forms (one with <r> and one with <s>; the former can also serve as a conditional in some contexts); except in very formal writing, the future subjunctive has now fallen out of use. In addition, the perfect aspect (used in preference to the preterite more often in Spain than in Latin America) can be formed with the auxiliary *haber* plus past participle without agreement (*han cantado* 'they have sung'); there is an immediate future with *ir a* 'go to' plus infinitive (*voy a cantar* 'I am going to sing'); and there is a progressive with *estar* 'be, stand' plus present participle (*están cantando* 'they are singing'). *Ser* 'be' is used with past participle agreement and the preposition *por* to form the passive (*fueron construidos aquí por los romanos* 'they were built here by the Romans'); the reflexive can often also be used with passive meaning (*Español se habla en Venezuela* 'Spanish is spoken in Venezuela').

Comparison is carried out either with *más* 'more' or *menos* 'less, fewer' plus *que* before an object or *de* before a number: *tengo menos que ella* 'I have fewer than her [she]'; *tengo más de dos* 'I have more than two'. Equative is with *tan(to)... como* 'as (many)... as'.

Adjectives agree with their nouns in all circumstances, typically placed after them (*una vergüenza terrible* 'a terrible disgrace'), but occasionally in front (in which case there may be modifications: *hombre grande* 'big man'; *gran_hombre* 'great man'). Adverbs are relatively rare, but in line with Vulgar Latin (3.4) may be formed adding *-mente* to the feminine form of the adjective (*rápido* 'quick', *rápidamente* 'quickly'); as with other Latin-derived languages, there are common irregulars (e.g. *bien* 'well'; *mal* 'badly').

Articles:

	Definite		Indefinite	
	Masculine	Feminine	Masculine	Feminine
Singular	*el*	*la (el)*	*un*	*una*
Plural	*los*	*las*	*unos*	*unas*

There is also a singular "neuter" article *lo,* used before adjectives standing alone: *lo importante es que te guste a ti* 'the important thing is that you like it'.

There is no elision but, before stressed initial *a-, la* rather confusingly switches to *el: el agua* 'the water' [feminine], *las aguas* 'the waters'.

Unlike in French and Italian (but, curiously, similarly to German), definite articles may also be used pronominally: *mi libro y el de mi hermana* 'my book and that of my sister'.

Plural indefinite articles are in relatively common use to mean 'some' or 'a number of': *unos cantantes* 'a number of singers'. Unlike in Portuguese and Italian, no definite article is required with possessive adjectives (9.3): *mi canción* 'my song' (although stylistically the article may be reinserted if the full possessive pronoun is placed after: *la canción mía* 'the song of mine').

Common prepositions:
- *de* 'of'; *a* 'to, at'; *por* 'for, by, through'; *para* 'for, towards'; *con* 'with' (note exceptional use with pronouns, 9.3); *en* 'in'.

The first two of these combine with the masculine singular definite article into a single word: *de+el=del* 'of the'; *a+el=al* 'to the'.

Spanish is notable for having some rarer prepositions which take a pronoun in its subject rather than prepositional (object) form: *entre tú y mi tío* 'between you and my uncle'; *según yo* 'according to me'.

Spanish tends to prefer nouns standing alone where other languages may prefer an adjective: *es verdad* 'it's true [it's truth]'.

Spanish is consistently a pro-drop language, meaning that verbs are used without the subject if the subject is clear: *canto* 'I sing'; *terminan* 'they finish'; *lo vimos* 'we saw it'. Personal pronouns only ever appear as subjects for emphasis.

Word order is typically SVO (SOV where the object is a pronoun), but it is in fact quite free and VSO is particularly common in questions (except in some Caribbean varieties) and in subordinate clauses (*el amigo que vieron los cantantes* 'the friend that the singers saw [the-friend-that-saw-the-singers]'). Unlike French and Italian, there is no "preceding direct object" agreement in modern Spanish in constructions with *haber*, but any object preceding the subject (or assumed subject if one is absent) must be repeated as an object pronoun (*esta canción la han escrito hoy* 'this song, they have written [it] today'; *este partido lo vamos a ganar* 'this game, we are going to win [it]'). The negative particle is *no*, placed before the verb and any object pronouns (*no la vimos* 'we did not see her'); with negative adverbs placed after the verb phrase there is double negation (*no la vimos nunca* 'we never saw her'; *no he hecho nada* 'I have not done anything') but negative adverbs placed in front stand alone (*tampoco la vimos* 'we did not see her either'; *nunca lo he hecho* 'I have never done it'); negative imperatives require the subjunctive (*¡no cantes!* 'do not sing!').

Yes/no questions rely merely on intonation:

- *canta* 'she sings'; *¿canta?* 'does she sing?'

Answer *sí* 'yes'; *no* 'no'.

9.5　Character

Modern Spanish is a generally vocalic language, but less so than Italian and with a somewhat flatter general intonation; this can vary, of course (indeed, the intonation of some varieties in Argentina and Uruguay can make them sound quite Italian to the untrained ear). It is also marked in all varieties by a soft, almost casual pronunciation of consonants.

Given its social and economic significance over such a wide area, Spanish is a comparatively and frustratingly under-studied language. Although there has been significant research into its socio-linguistic situation (notably where it encounters and exists alongside other languages, such as in California, Catalonia, Paraguay and elsewhere), detailed academic research into aspects of its vocabulary, phonology and grammar is often lacking.

Spanish (in all varieties) allows for a huge range of subtly different choices in vocabulary, word order and verb form, enabling nuanced expression which is rarely catered for in detail in any textbook, but which is fundamental to developing a complete grasp of the character of the language and of the diverse cultures in which it is spoken.

Spanish displays a clear focus on verbs, often preferring complex verb forms or even nouns turned into verbs (e.g. *necesitar* 'need', *solucionar* 'sort out') to clauses focused on nouns.

Padre nuestro, que estás en el cielo, santificado sea tu nombre; venga a nosotros tu reino; hágase tu voluntad en la tierra como en el cielo; danos hoy nuestro pan de cada día; perdona nuestras ofensas, como también nosotros perdonamos a los que nos ofenden; no nos dejes caer en tentación, y líbranos del mal.

10

FRENCH

Of Latin origin but markedly distinct due to early Germanic influence and subsequently rapid pronunciation change, French is a remarkable language in every sense. Spoken natively by fewer than 125 million souls, thus ahead in that regard only of Italian among the major national Western European languages derived from Latin, it nevertheless retains a global influence well beyond its numbers and an international prestige among modern languages which is arguably unparalleled.

French took over from Latin in the modern era as the language of the elite (it was spoken in most European Royal Courts for centuries) and of the educated. From international treaties to global post, French remains instantly recognizable and widespread in diplomacy and high culture. It is the foremost administrative language in the United Nations and the European institutions besides English, and it is a *lingua franca* across most of North Africa. Although less prominently than Spanish or Portuguese, it has also gone trans-Atlantic, as it is also spoken natively in parts of the Caribbean and (with marked differences in pronunciation and colloquial vocabulary) in the Canadian provinces of Quebec and New Brunswick.

Linguistically, French is also outstanding. It largely retains its Medieval spelling system, but pronunciation has developed dramatically. This disconnect between the written and spoken language causes significant complexity, particularly concerning how words are pronounced differently depending on their environment.

10.1   Phonology

French phonology is a linguistic phenomenon, having developed far further from Latin than any other major language. Arising from the reduction and often complete elimination of sounds, a hugely complex system of "liaison" exists (rules governing how sequences of sounds crossing word boundaries are pronounced).

French is free of many harsh or rarer sounds. Thus, for many learners, the initial challenge is its strong and distinctive nasalization. Like many aspects of the language, the distinction between the pronunciation of the four main nasals (generally written <an>, <en>, <in> and <on> as well as occasionally <un>, with any following dental consonant <t> or <d> generally silent) is contested even by native speakers and exhibits an ongoing pronunciation shift. Some speakers now pronounce many of the low and central nasals similarly, so that *grand* 'big', *vent* 'wind' and *ton* 'your' seem to rhyme, although this is frowned upon by many (and most still do distinguish *vent*).

Modern French is also noted for a series of once complex but now reduced vowel combinations (*lieu* 'place'; *chevaux* 'horses'; *moi* 'me'; *haie* 'hedge'). These have changed swiftly through time, and they are often pronounced more conservatively in Canada.

However, the stand-out feature is liaison. Except when liaison applies, most final consonants (though not all) are left silent in most instances. An extreme example is the number *six*, once pronounced not far from its modern English equivalent, whose final letter now has three pronunciations – *j'en ai six* 'I have six' (/s/); *six amis* 'six friends' (/z/); *six voyageurs* 'six travellers' (silent). Three is unusual, but most words ending in a consonant (in writing) do have two pronunciations – a citation form with the final consonant silent, and a liaison form with the final consonant sounded. When sounded, final consonants are consistently pronounced specifically as either the voiced or voiceless version – so <t> or <d> is always pronounced /t/; <s>, <x> or <z> is /z/; etc. However, the rules of exactly when they may or must be sounded are complex (and have changed through time): for example, there is liaison after *comment* in *comment allez-vous?* 'how are you?' but not in *comment est-elle arrivée?* 'how did she arrive?'

Related to this also is the concept of *enchaînement,* which sees the final consonant before an initial vowel in effect pronounced as if it were part of the following word. Conventions also dictate when a final -*e* is silent or sounded: typically, in modern speech it is silent, but in combinations of words it may reappear in one: *une grande femme* 'a great woman' [in this case, final -*e* sounded only in *grande*].

Another marked development is the switch of initial <c> in Latin to an affricate, written <ch>: *cheval* 'horse'; *chaine* 'chain'. This once had the initial stop sound /t/ as in English but has since lost it (thus, it was formerly pronounced as if English <ch> but in the modern language is pronounced as if English <sh>; compare 'chief' borrowed from Old French with 'chef', originally the same word, borrowed centuries later).

French is pronounced towards the front of the mouth (though <r> is trilled towards the back) with a distinctive even stress – syllables are all the same length and carry roughly the same emphasis. In Europe, it is generally spoken with a rising intonation; in Canadian and some African varieties this may be less apparent.

10.2   Standard

Founded in 1635, the *Academie Française* is perhaps the most famous language institute in the world, charged with determining (and promoting) what is and what is not Standard French. Within the French-speaking world (known as *la Francophonie*), this standard form is perhaps of higher prestige than is typical with other languages, with regional (or any other) variations less tolerated. As ever, this applies primarily to the written language, but often also to spoken French. Particularly in France itself, debate can become remarkably philosophical over the rules of liaison, general standards of eloquence, and other matters of pronunciation and usage. There is also a significant degree of purism, with resistance to borrowings from other languages.

Spelling is based on the French spoken in Paris after the Black Death of the mid 14th century (as is, coincidentally, the case with English). This was not necessarily easily understood even across the rest of northern France at the time, and it was quite alien in the south. Even at the time of the French Revolution in the late 18th century, a huge range of often mutually unintelligible dialects existed across the country; there is evidence that a combination of nationalism and centralization in the decades after the Revolution saw these quickly eclipsed and the standard language come to predominate, often even in speech (whereas this generally only happened with most other European languages after the invention of broadcasting).

As noted at 10.1, a consequence of the spelling system of this standard form being based on the speech of so long ago, alongside the remarkable phonological development of the language, has been an astonishing and in fact unstable disconnect between the spoken and written language. Spelling is relatively (though not completely) consistent; however, guessing spelling purely from pronunciation is often impossible. This, combined with the complex rules of liaison, makes French an outstandingly hard language to master absolutely – arguably even for its own native speakers!

Written accents in French are: the acute (only *é*) to mark an open pronunciation; the grave (*è*) to mark closed, or on other letters to mark distinction (*où* 'where', *ou* 'or'; *là* 'there', *la* 'the'); the controversial and often now optional circumflex on vowels to mark distinction (*dû* 'had to', *du* 'of the') or a historical following <s> (*hôtel*) or <a> (*âge*); the diaresis to mark separate pronunciation of vowels written in combination (*naïve*); and the cedilla, which originally marked a <z> but is now used to mark soft <c> before a low vowel (now pronounced /s/; *ça* 'that'). Additionally, abbreviated forms of pronouns ending -*e* are compulsory, with apostrophes replacing the *e* in all forms of writing where they are followed by vowels or silent *h*-; *ce+est=c'est* 'this is', *je+ai=j'ai* 'I have'; this has not been extended to pronouns ending in other vowels, although forms such as **t'as* (Standard *tu as)* 'you have' are seen increasingly in informal writing.

10.3   Vocabulary

French vocabulary is predominantly drawn from Late Latin (including Greek borrowings during the Classical period) and thus is aligned heavily with Spanish, Portuguese and most notably Italian.

Key numbers:
1 un, 2 deux, 3 trois, 4 quatre, 5 cinq, 6 six, 7 sept, 8 huit, 9 neuf;
10 dix, 11 onze, 12 douze, 15 quinze, 16 seize, 17 dix-sept;
20 vingt, 21 vingt et un, 26 vingt-six; 46 quarante-six; 66 soixante-six;
76 soixante-seize; 96 quatre-vingt-seize; 100 cent; 1000 mille;
456789 quatre cent cinquante-six mille sept cent quatre-vingt-neuf.

Above 60, this demonstrates a vigesimal (twenty-based) counting system probably borrowed from the Normans, who were originally Norse (Old Norse exhibited some similar patterns which are retained in Modern Danish, 12.3).

In Belgian, Congolese and Swiss French, this vigesimal system is largely ignored, with *70 septante* and *90 nonante* (occasionally in some Swiss dialects even *80 huitante*) preferred.

However, there are two noteworthy differences. First, as noted at 10.1, French phonology is heavily reduced, meaning it is not always obvious which words are related (e.g. *chaine* 'chain'; Spanish *cadena*, Latin/Italian *catena*). Second, what became modern French was influenced much earlier by another major language (the West Germanic which became German, Dutch and English), which provided a range of non-Latin vocabulary in certain areas such as orienteering (*nord* 'north'), colours (*bleu* 'blue'), or warfare (*guerre* 'war') – some of this was later further borrowed into other Latin-derived languages.

Personal pronouns (masculine/feminine):

	Singular (1st, 2nd, 3rd)			Plural (1st, 2nd, 3rd)		
Subject	*je*	*tu*	*il/elle*			*ils/elles*
Object	*me*	*te*	*le/la*	*nous*	*vous*	*les*
Prepositional	*moi*	*toi*	*lui/elle*			*eux/elles*

Possessive adjectives (masculine/feminine):

Singular	*mon/ma*	*ton/ta*	*son/sa*	*notre*	*votre*	*leur*
Plural	*mes*	*tes*	*ses*	*nos*	*vos*	*leurs*

Possessive pronouns (masculine/feminine):

Singular	*mien/mienne*	*tien*	*sien*	*nôtre*	*vôtre*	*leur*
Plural	*miens/miennes*	etc.	etc.	*nôtres*	*vôtres*	*leurs*

Lui (for both genders) and *leur* are also used as indirect object forms: *je le leur ai donné* 'I have given it to them'. Reflexive forms are the same as object except third person *se*.

Vous is also used as the polite second person singular (with plural verb forms).

Modern spoken French also makes widespread use of the subject pronoun *on* (prepositional *soi*), originally cognate with *homme* 'man' and equivalent to English 'one', but often used in preference to *nous* or occasionally *je* or *tu* where these have a general meaning; it is used with a third person singular verb form but adjectives agree according to how many people are being referred to: *on est arrivées* 'we have arrived / one has [singular] arrived [feminine plural]'.

French also has a specific locative pronoun *y* (for place) and genitive *en* (for belonging): *je l'y avais vue* 'I had seen her there'; *vous en avez trois* 'you have three of them'.

The demonstrative adjective is (masculine/feminine) singular *ce(t)/cette,* plural *ces;* the pronoun is singular *celui/celle*, plural *ceux/celles*. Only one grade is used in general, but this may be reinforced by adding the particle *-ci* 'this, these/' or *-là* 'that, those' (from *ici* 'here'; *là* 'there'): *ce mois-ci* 'this month'; *cette année-là* 'that year'; *cet hôtel* 'this/that hotel', *celles-là* 'those ones [fem.]'.

Relative pronouns: *qui* (subject), *que* (object), *dont* (genitive); *l'homme qui l'a vue* 'the man who saw her', *l'homme qu'elle a vu* 'the man she saw', *l'homme dont elle parle* 'the man she speaks of'.

Interrogative pronouns: *quoi* 'what', *quand* 'when', *où* 'where', *comment* 'how', *quel/quelle(s)* 'which'. Relative pronouns may also be used for questions. Particularly in speech *qu'est-ce* is effectively now a question marker: *qu'est-ce qu'il a vu?* 'what did he see?'

10.4   Grammar

French nouns are (usually) marked for the plural in writing and are inherently masculine or feminine. Old French retained a case system for a lot longer than most other Latin-derived languages; masculine nouns added *-s* to mark singular subject or plural object; feminine nouns simply added *-s* to mark any plural. Early in the second millennium this came to be regularized in line with the latter and *-s* became solely a plural marker (though vestiges of the old masculine singular ending remain in personal names such as *Georges* or *Jacques*, and in some exceptional forms such as *fils* 'son'), with the exception that where the ending was once *-ls* this is now written *-(u)x*. Nouns ending *-s*, *-x* or *-z* in the singular are unmarked in the plural (*nez* 'nose, noses'). In speech, this plural marker is no longer pronounced in most instances; the plural is made clear from the surrounding words.

Verb endings of *chanter* 'sing', (*-a-* stem; 1st, 2nd, 3rd person).

Present indicative ('sing'):
- singular *chante, chantes, chante;*
- plural *chantons, chantez, chantent.*

These were taken over from Late Latin and were once clearly distinct from each other in speech except in the first and third person singular, with endings fully pronounced (note <z> was once pronounced /ts/ as in German). However, in spoken French even the third person plural is now identical to the singular forms (i.e. the ending itself is not pronounced). The present subjunctive is the same as the indicative, except first and second person plural *chantions, chantiez;* it is distinct in all persons only with common verbs (e.g. *faire* 'do', *être* 'be') or a particular set ending in *-ir* (e.g. *finir* 'finish, end').

Imperfect ('used to sing'):
- singular *chantais, chantais, chantait;*
- plural *chantions, chantiez, chantaient.*

Future ('will sing'):
- singular *chanterai, chanteras, chantera;*
- plural *chanterons, chanterez, chanteront.*

Conditional ('would sing'):
- singular *chanterais, chanterais, chanterait;*
- plural *chanterions, chanteriez, chanteraient.*

Imperative ('sing!'):
- singular *chante*; plural *chantez.*

Notably, in speech, only the future distinguishes between first, second and third person singular and third person plural – in all other tenses these are pronounced alike; as are the infinitive *chanter* and the past participle *chanté* (there is also a present participle *chantant*).

French verbs can be marked for future, conditional or imperfect (the latter most usually with common verbs); the preterite has become restricted to formal writing so that past reference otherwise is generally carried out via the perfect, which requires auxiliaries (*avoir* 'have' or *être* 'be'; the latter requires subject-participle agreement) and the past participle: *j'ai chanté* 'I have sung'; *elles sont allées* 'they have gone'. The passive is formed identically with *être* (and preposition *par*): *elle est vue par toi* 'she is seen by you'. The present and past subjunctive, while rarer than in the other major Latin-derived languages and indistinguishable from the indicative in many instances even in writing, remains in common use. The auxiliary *aller* 'go' may be used with an infinitive for immediate future reference: *je vais chanter* 'I am going to sing'. There is no specific progressive construction, however; other idiomatic expressions are required to indicate continuous action.

Uniquely among major Latin-derived languages, French is absolutely not pro-drop; every sentence must have a subject, even if it is a dummy subject: *tu chantes* 'you sing'; *ils finissent* 'they finish'; *nous l'avons vu* 'we saw it'; *il pleut* 'it is raining'.

Where other Latin-derived languages re-insert the subject pronoun for emphasis, spoken French uses an additional prepositional (object) form: _moi, je ne l'ai pas vu_ 'I [emphasized] did not see it'.

Adjectives agree with their noun for gender and number in all circumstances. The feminine form adds _-e_ in writing (occasionally with other modifications: _beau/belle_ 'beautiful', _neuf/neuve_ 'new'), which is itself not generally pronounced but has the effect of sounding the final consonant (which, though written, is typically dropped in speech in the masculine form: _grand/grande_ 'big, great'; 10.1). They are generally placed after the noun, but may appear before, including with subtle variations in meaning (as in Spanish, 9.4): _un grand homme_ 'a great man'; _un homme grand_ 'a big man'.

Articles:

	Definite		Indefinite	
	Masculine	Feminine	Masculine	Feminine
Singular	_le (l')_	_la (l')_	_un_	_une_
Plural	_les_		_des_	

Definite articles of both genders are reduced to _l'_ before vowels (or silent _h-_). As in Italian (7.4), there is also in effect a further singular partitive article (masculine _du_, feminine _de la_); this is used for general quantities (but, unlike in Italian, it is considered compulsory; the noun cannot appear alone): _du pain_ 'some bread', _de la chance_ 'some luck', _des pommes_ 'some apples'. Possessives do not require an article but agree in gender with the noun (rather than the possessor): _son père_ 'his/her father'; _sa mère_ 'his/her mother'; _notre chanson_ 'our song'; the masculine form is used, however, even with feminine nouns if they begin with a vowel or silent _h-_: _mon histoire_ 'my story' [feminine].

Common prepositions:
* _de_ 'of, from'; _à_ 'to, at'; _en_ 'in, at'; _avec_ 'with'; _pour_ 'for'; _par_ 'by, through'; _vers_ 'towards'; _chez_ 'at the home of'.

The first two merge with the definite article to form a single word in the plural _(des, aux)_ and masculine singular _(du, au)_.

French has developed an unusual form of mandatory double negation, with the particle *ne* placed before the main verb and a further particle (most commonly *pas*) almost always required directly after it: *tu ne chantes pas* 'you do not sing'; *je n'ai rien fait* 'I have not done anything'; *il ne pleut plus* 'it is no longer raining'. In speech, the *ne* is frequently dropped.

Parisian French in fact adopted Germanic word order late in the first millennium (V2, so verb second element regardless of first element; 13.4), which was replaced in written French by SVO (SOV in most instances where the object is a pronoun) gradually from around the 15th century, perhaps under the influence of the southern Latin-derived dialects it displaced as it gradually became the language of the whole of France. In practice, word order is flexible in spoken French and some vestiges of Germanic influence remain even in formal written usage: *peut-être est elle là* 'perhaps she is there [perhaps-is-she-there]'. French also adopted a system of "preceding direct object" agreement in the formation of the perfect, whereby a past participle agrees with its direct object if the object appears before it: *tu l'avais vue* 'you had seen her'; *les chansons que nous avons écrites* 'the songs we wrote'.

Yes/no questions may be by inversion (often with the insertion of *-t-* to aid pronunciation) but tend, particularly in speech, to be restructured using *est-ce-que* 'is this that' effectively as a question marker:
- *elle chante* 'she sings';
- *chante-t-elle? / est-ce qu'elle chante?* 'does she sing?'

Answer *oui* 'yes', *non* 'no'; *si* 'yes [to a negative]'.

10.5   Character

French is closest to Italian among the four major national Western European languages derived from Latin, although it is still in practice more distant from it than any of the other three is from any other. It does share Italian's slight preference for noun-based constructions compared to Spanish and Portuguese.

In speech, modern French is marked by little evident stress within or even between words, particularly in European varieties. This is exceptionally hard for non-native speakers to master (and generally not enough work is done on it by teachers and tutors, as it is essential to good comprehension); conversely, it marks French speakers out when they speak other languages.

The profound influence from Germanic on French (vestiges of which appear both in vocabulary, 10.3, and word order, 10.4) cannot be underestimated; even the name 'France' (for the Franks, hence also Frankfurt, Franconia etc) is of Germanic origin. This explains much of its distinctiveness from any other language.

French is also marked by a tendency to add or maintain particles (particularly in speech), which is perhaps a consequence of having reduced so many sounds, syllables and words. Therefore, although in speech French words are individually often shorter than in Portuguese, Spanish or particularly Italian, there may be additions to clauses and sentences which have the effect of re-lengthening them: e.g. Spanish *¿qué es?* and Italian *cos'è?* become French *qu'est-ce que c'est?* 'what is it? [what-is-this-that-this-is?]'

French is notably vocalic (though perhaps still not quite as much so as Italian), and thus excellent for music.

Notre Père, qui es aux cieux, que ton nom soit sanctifié; que ton règne vienne, que ta volonté soit faite sur la terre comme au ciel. Donne-nous aujourd'hui notre pain de ce jour. Pardonne-nous nos offences, comme nous pardonnons aussi à ceux qui nous ont offensés. Et ne nous laisse pas entrer en tentation, mais délivre-nous du mal.

11

———

LATINATE LANGUAGES

All contemporary "Italic" languages derive from Vulgar Latin. This had already split into distinct local vernaculars over 2000 years ago and ultimately developed into clearly different languages from around the eighth century, but it bears emphasizing that almost half the changes between Classical Latin and any modern standard national language derived from it had already happened by the time of this split.

The terminology is complex here because although there is a branch of Indo-European simply called "Germanic", the branch which includes Latin is sometimes called "Italic", "Latinate" or most commonly with reference to modern languages "Romance". Classical Latin itself was an "Italic" language, which refers to a group of languages which was clearly distinct from other branches of Indo-European by the time they arrived in Italy. Languages derived from Latin itself are often referred to as "Latinate" (to specify the link to Latin) or as "Romance" (for "Rome").

Very broadly, we can split the modern Latinate languages in this book into "Iberian" (Spanish and Portuguese) and "Italo-Gallic" (French and Italian), at least in their standard varieties. Nevertheless, largely because of its dramatic phonological development (and also the subsequent impact on grammar), French is the outlier – although Italian is geographically and in some ways idiomatically closer to French, from the learner's point of view it will be perceived grammatically and phonologically as closer to the Iberian languages.

One significant difference between "Iberian" and "Italo-Gallic" is in vocabulary. Latin arrived in Iberia well before its Golden Age, and thus before significant borrowing from Greek. For example, the Early Latin verb *fābulārī* has become Portuguese *falar,* Spanish *hablar* 'speak'; however, French *parler* and Italian *parlare* (indeed even Esperanto *paroli*) derive from a later Greek borrowing.

Phonologically, all Latin-derived languages broadly prefer soft sounds; they are more vocalic than Classical Latin was; and they exhibit significant changes to pronunciation of vowels and letters such as <c> and <g> (which have softened, albeit in differing ways, before high vowels usually written <e> or <i>). There have been some divergences, particularly in the simplification of clusters, loss of medial letters (i.e. consonants surrounded by vowels or vice-versa) and voicing of consonants. French has moved the fastest with its remarkably complex system of reduction and consequent liaison (10.1); it is followed by Spanish and Portuguese and then by Italian, whose standard is the most conservative form (i.e. closest to Latin). Generally, all syllables in contemporary Latinate languages are the same length in speech (although Continental Portuguese has quite distinct vowel lengthening and stress; 8.1), and pronunciation is towards the front of the mouth.

The modern Latinate languages in this book have all reduced three genders to two, continuing to mark them on words surrounding or referring to the noun; and they exhibit agreement of the adjective with the noun in all circumstances (and in each language adjectives generally follow nouns, with some minor exceptions). Their most interesting collective grammatical feature is perhaps their treatment of the verb, however; verbs are consistently marked for three tenses (past, present and future) plus the conditional. These three tenses are assumed to be "normal" by many people across the Western world, but actually they are a clear marker of Latin-derived languages (as discussed in later chapters, Germanic languages actually only have two tenses; many other languages globally do not primarily mark tense at all). Additionally, most Latin-derived languages continue to differentiate between imperfect and perfect aspect in the past. Through use of auxiliaries (usually those meaning or derived from 'be' and 'have', or occasionally 'stand', 'go' and 'come'), a wide range of tense and aspect combinations is available. Notably, even though it has receded in some, all Latinate languages continue to mark the subjunctive mood to some extent even in informal speech, at least in the present and the past. None marks for case (preferring prepositions instead) except with some pronouns; and notably all have a fundamentally SVO word order except if the object is a pronoun, in which case they are usually SOV.

This book has not, of course, covered a fifth significant national Latinate language, namely Romanian, nor some other important national and regional languages such as Catalan, Romansh and Sardinian. Completely isolated geographically from other Latin-derived languages, the prime distinct grammatical features of Romanian are that the definite article follows the noun and it maintains a separate genitive-dative case; it also derives significant vocabulary and some grammatical forms from neighbouring Slavic languages. Catalan is significantly reduced phonologically (although not to the same extent as Standard French), exhibits some distinction in the use of articles and the form of some prepositions (e.g. *amb* 'with'), and has a notable feature in its verbal system whereby *anar* 'go' as an auxiliary marks past rather than future. Romansh is often grouped with Ladin and Friulian to form a distinct set of Alpine languages of Latin origin (though this grouping is disputed), notable phonologically for the maintenance of long versus short vowels. Sardinian is the most conservative Latin-derived language of all, maintaining even the hard <c> (i.e. /k/) sound from Classical Latin in all circumstances.

Because much language study in the English-speaking world has been focused on the Classics, a lot of assumptions about languages in general are made based on Latin – which is peculiar, because English is a Germanic, not a Latinate, language. Notions such as three tenses, two genders, subjunctives, object pronouns preceding verbs and so on are indeed common to a lot of the first languages English speakers learn (most obviously Spanish and French), but they are not in fact the norm and they are not a feature of Germanic languages such as English itself.

12

SCANDINAVIAN (DANISH)

Modern Germanic languages are grouped by historical relationship into "North" and "West" branches – "East", represented most notably by Gothic (Chapter 4), has gone extinct. Since the focus of this handbook is on Western rather than Northern European languages, it is also on West rather than North Germanic. However, given their common origins, it is worth looking briefly at North Germanic for comparison.

The North Germanic language family excludes Finnish, which is not Indo-European at all, but otherwise includes all the languages of the Nordic countries. Historically, these too were split between Western (broadly Norwegian, Faroese and Icelandic) and Eastern (broadly Swedish and Danish). However, although exact groupings and terminology can vary, nowadays the more meaningful split is generally considered to be between Insular (Icelandic and Faroese) and Scandinavian (Norwegian, Danish and Swedish).

In terms of language politics, Norwegian is a peculiar case without obvious parallel. Over centuries of rule from Copenhagen, the language of administration in Norway came effectively to be Danish (albeit spoken with a Norwegian accent and generally referred to in Norway as "Norwegian"). Over time, this was also adopted by educated speakers in Norway, particularly in the more urban east. However, in rural and coastal areas, traditional spoken dialects were barely influenced at all by Danish, and they remained more typically western (thus retaining more similarities with insular languages like

Icelandic). Upon independence, language standardization became a significant political issue and Norway was ultimately left with no option but to adopt two "standards" – one representing the traditional rural and coastal dialects known as *Nynorsk* 'New Norwegian'; and another largely representative of the previous administrative language, initially referred to as "Dano-Norwegian" but officially known as *Bokmål* 'Book Tongue'. The latter is predominant in writing, but both retain equal official status nationally.

Of the populations of the three largest Scandinavian countries, Norwegians are most used to dialect variation (even internally) and are thus typically the best at understanding either of the other two. Broadly, Norwegian (at least in variants close to the *Bokmål* standard) is closer to Danish in writing but to Swedish in speech. Danes and Swedes can struggle to understand each other's spoken languages, although there is some mutual intelligibility particularly between eastern Danish and southern Swedish dialects (either side of the Oresund). Scandinavians generally have little difficulty reading each other's languages.

Most Scandinavians also speak excellent English, to the extent that interviews in English are occasionally shown on television in Nordic countries with neither subtitles nor dubbing felt necessary. Despite the large degree of mutual intelligibility between Scandinavian languages, particularly in writing, English is often the preferred language of communication across Scandinavian borders.

Swedish is the major Scandinavian language – its 10 million speakers account for around half the total. However, the nearest to Western Europe (and the one with the most interesting phonological development) is Danish, so it is the focus here.

12.1 Phonology

Among Germanic languages, Danish is remarkably phonologically reduced (to a similar extent as French among Latin-derived languages; 10.1). Perhaps the most noteworthy feature of its pronunciation is *stød*, whereby syllables may be separated by a "creaky voice", a break feature similar to but not quite the same as a soft glottal stop (often accompanied by an apparent change in pitch). This is not always reflected in writing: *læser* 'read(s)' (the verb form) exhibits *stød* before the *-er* suffix, but *læser* 'reader' does not. No one quite knows how or when this developed (although it was certainly apparent by the 16th century), and it is not present in some traditional southern dialects.

Danish also vocalizes some consonants after vowels: *dag* 'day' (pronounced similarly to English 'die'), *skov* 'forest'. Vowels themselves can be long or short, and there are numerous diphthongs.

Another notable feature of Danish phonology is the softness of consonants (voiced consonants are frequently softened to become devoiced and those which were initially devoiced are then softened further), particularly medially: the first syllable of the verb in *jeg hedder* 'I am called' is not much different from English 'hell', and the <b> in *at købe* 'to buy' is close to /w/.

The Danes are said to speak with "a potato in their throat", and the location of articulation at the back of the mouth but perhaps a little higher than other Germanic languages would in some ways explain that. As noted above, stressed syllables are often conditioned by "breaking", giving the language a strikingly unusual sound.

12.2   Standard

Danish was distinct from Swedish by the time it began to be written down from the late 12th century (until then the administrative language of Denmark, which at the time included part of what is now southern Sweden, was in fact Latin).

Particularly from the 17th century, Danes played a disproportionate role in the development of the field of linguistics itself. Gradually they codified a standard for their own language, based generally on the form used in government and therefore on the educated dialect of Copenhagen. The most recent significant spelling reform was in 1948.

Nevertheless, rapid changes in pronunciation in the last few centuries mean that several common words (notably some personal pronouns) are still spelled irregularly.

The Danish alphabet adds the letters *æ, å* and *ø*, which often mark the equivalent of umlaut (i.e. are grammatically distinctive). Officially, clauses must be separated by commas as in German, but in practice usage varies.

12.3   Vocabulary

Danish (and, broadly, Scandinavian) vocabulary is overwhelmingly Germanic, deriving fundamentally from the Norse spoken by the Vikings.

However, it was reinforced by significant borrowings from Low German, the ancestor of traditional dialects sometimes still spoken in rural northern Germany and parts of the Netherlands (now somewhere between modern Standard German and Standard Dutch). This influence was primarily due to trade in the Middle Ages, meaning that terminology in commerce, navigation and local administration is often similar to German or Dutch (with the Norse-derived terms displaced).

An outstanding feature of Danish is its numbering system, which displays the vigesimal (i.e. twenty-based) system used by the Vikings – Danish is the only modern Scandinavian language which retains it. This means that higher numbers are expressed not by the number of tens, but by the number of twenties; this includes halves, and halves are counted to the next whole: for example, in effect 90 is based on 'half-to-five-times-twenty' (i.e. $4\frac{1}{2} \times 20$).

Key numbers:
1 en/et, 2 to, 3 tre, 4 fire, 5 fem, 6 seks, 7 syv, 8 otte, 9 ni;
10 ti, 11 elleve, 12 tolv, 15 femten, 16 seksten, 17 sytten;
20 tyve, 21 enogtyve, 30 tredive, 40 fyrre, 50 halvtreds, 60 tres,
70 halvfjerds, 80 firs, 90 halvfems; 100 hundrede; 1000 tusind;
456789 fire hundrede seksoghalvtreds tusind syv hundrede niogfirs.

SCANDINAVIAN (DANISH)

Swedish and Norwegian now use a ten-based counting system and place tens before units as in English: thus 92 is *nittiotvå* ['ninetytwo'] in Swedish but *tooghalvfems* ['two-and-half-(to)-five'] in Danish.

In the modern language, there is little resistance to borrowings from English (given the high proficiency Scandinavians generally have in it), including even occasionally of entire phrases.

Personal pronouns (masculine/feminine):

	Singular (1st, 2nd, 3rd)			Plural (1st, 2nd, 3rd)		
Subject	*jeg*	*du*	*han/hun*	*vi*	*I*	*de*
Object	*mig*	*dig*	*ham/hende*	*os*	*jer*	*dem*

In the singular third person, *han/hun* and *ham/hende* specifically refer to people (masculine/feminine); otherwise, *den/det* are used (both subject and object) as impersonal pronouns, coded for the gender of the referent (common/neuter). Reflexive forms are the same as object forms except third person (singular and plural) *sig*.

Possessive pronouns/adjectives (masculine/feminine):

Common	*min*	*din*				
Neuter	*mit*	*dit*	*hans/hendes*	*vores*	*jeres*	*deres*
Plural	*mine*	*dine*				

As above, *hans/hendes* 'his/her(s)' specifically refer to people; *dens/dets* 'its' are used as impersonal possessives, coded for the gender of the possessor (common/neuter).

In the third person possessive, the reflexive series *sin-sit-sine* replaces *hans/hendes/dens/dets* or *deres* if the reference is to the subject: *han har hans bog* 'he has his [someone else's] book'; *han har sin bog* 'he has his (own) book'.

Vores may also decline in formal writing (as *vor-vort-vore*), but now rarely does so in the spoken language or in informal contexts.

Danish did use *De/Dem* as polite second person forms for both singular and plural, but these suddenly fell out of general use in the early 1970s and are now encountered only in the most formal writing.

Interrogative pronouns:
- *hvem* 'who', *hvad* 'what', *hvilken* 'which', *hvor* 'where';
- *hvornår* 'when', *hvordan* 'how', *hvorfor* 'why'.

Relative pronouns:
- Interrogatives, plus *som* 'what', *der* 'who, which'.

12.4   Grammar

In the standard language, Danish nouns may be one of two genders (common or neuter). The plural is generally marked in *-er* (*sted-steder* 'place-places'), with another smaller group of short words in *-e* (*hund-hunde* 'dog-dogs'); some others form the plural by change of root vowel, either with or without the ending (*mand-mænd* 'man-men', *bog-bøger* 'book-books'); and a few are unmarked (*dyr-dyr* 'animal-animals'). However, in the absence of any preposition (in some instances), adjective or determiner, any definite article which appears is joined to the noun as a suffix: common *-(e)n*, neuter *-(e)t* and plural *-ne* (*hund* 'dog', *hunden* 'the dog', *hunde* 'dogs', *hundene* 'the dogs'). There are no case markings in modern Danish, although possession is marked by a clitic *-s* (*min fars hus* 'my father's house').

In Swedish and Norwegian, the definite article suffix appears even where the noun is supported by an adjective or determiner: Danish *det gamle hus*, Norwegian *det gamle huset* 'the old house'.

Both Norwegian Standards maintain three genders; Standard Swedish has just two (common and neuter), as in Standard Danish.

Danish main verbs, fundamentally, are marked for present in *-(e)r*; or past, generally in *-te* or *-de* (although as in other Germanic languages there is a group of "strong" verbs which mark their past forms by changing the root vowel). Notably, verbs are not marked to agree with their subject in any modern Scandinavian language (i.e. the verb form is the same for all three persons, singular and plural). There is also a specific habitual passive marker (which can be added to past or present), *-es*: *bogen læses* 'the book is read [generally]'. Verbs also have participle forms (typically in *-t*), which may be used with the common irregular verbs *at være* 'to be' or more commonly *at blive* 'to become' to form a passive (used typically for one-off action: *bogen bliver læst* 'the book is read [once]'); or with *at have* 'to have' to form the perfect aspect (for relevant completed action: *jeg har læst bogen* 'I have read the book'). Aside from in archaic or set phrases, there is no distinct subjunctive/conjunctive mood in modern Danish.

Key prepositions:
- *på* 'to, at', *til* 'to, for'; *i* 'in'; *af* 'of'; *med* 'with'; *mod* 'against'.

As in most Germanic languages, adverbs are unmarked. Adjectives, however, have varying forms depending on whether they are used attributively (in which case they are placed before the noun) or predicatively and, in the former case, what their environment is. In most circumstances (when indefinite or used predicatively) adjectives agree with their noun by adding *-t* for the neuter singular or *-e* for plurals (there is no change for the common singular): *en stor bog* 'a big book', *et stort hus* 'a big house', *store bøger* 'big books'; *bogen er stor* 'the book is big', *huset bliver stort* 'the house gets big'. Definite attributive adjectives always add *-e*: *den store bog* 'the big book', *det store hus* 'the big house'. Generally, no *-e* is required with adjectives already ending in a vowel; some adjectives also display other irregular modifications. In practice, this means adjectives often appear in the form with the *-t* ending in general use, because after *det* 'that' the neuter form is required: *det er fint* 'that is fine'.

Comparison is by way of the ending *-(e)re* with the conjunction *end*: *dette mesterskab er vigtigere end et spil* 'this championship is more important than one game' (but longer adjectives may instead use *mere*: *mere intelligent* 'more intelligent'). The pejorative uses determiner *mindre*: *dette mesterskab er mindre vigtigt* 'this championship is less important'; equative uses *så ... som* 'as ... as'.

Scandinavian languages are fundamentally SVO and V2, meaning that the verb phrase stands as the second element in the clause (excluding conjunctions), regardless of what the first element is. This is the case even if the first element is itself a clause: *da jeg boede i det hus, havde jeg hunde* 'when I lived in that house, I had dogs [when-I-lived-in-that-house-had-I-dogs]'. The negative particle *ikke* generally follows the verb: *jeg havde ikke hunde* 'I did not have dogs'.

Yes/no questions are by inversion:
* *hun synger* 'she sings'; *synger hun?* 'does she sing?'

Answer *ja* 'yes', *nej* 'no'; *jo* 'yes [to a negative]'.

12.5   Character

In general, Scandinavian languages initially appear quintessentially Germanic, with the focus placed firmly on nouns. They have also had significant influence on and from West Germanic languages. However, the distinct origins of much of their core vocabulary and their comparatively regularized grammatical structure does mean that, when looked at in detail, they stand quite apart from continental West Germanic languages, and particularly from German.

Danish specifically is noted for its remarkable phonology; it can almost appear as if words are scarcely pronounced at all. Conversely Swedish, and to a lesser extent Norwegian, stand out among Western European languages for their almost tonal system of pronunciation.

Fader vor, du som er i Himlene, helliget vorde dit navn, komme dit rige, ske din vilje, som i Himlen, således også på jorden. Giv os i dag vort daglige brød, og forlad os vor skyld, som også vi forlader vore skyldnere. Og led os ikke ind i fristelse, men fri os fra det onde.

13

——

GERMAN

German is the most published language in the world after English, and knowledge of it is a huge benefit for anyone wanting to carry out in-depth study in a range of subjects from philosophy to linguistics itself. It is also the most spoken native language in Europe and has long been established as a significant trading language. Currently, only English and Chinese speakers export more than German speakers.

German is, however, both seemingly somewhat alien (with its conservative grammar and limited Latin influence) and harsh sounding (with its hard consonants and glottal stops). It is also perceived to be considerably more structurally complex than other contemporary major Western European languages. This can make German more challenging at the outset but ultimately, as with any language, a combination of determination and focusing on the right correspondences can make the task easier.

13.1   Phonology

German exhibits some harsh consonantal sounds, most notably that written <ch> (*Loch* 'hole', similar to Scottish 'lo*ch*'). However, the phonology is relatively accessible for speakers of most other Western European languages. The vowels are comparatively simple, the diphthongs uncomplicated (though <ai> and <ei> are pronounced alike in the modern language), and most consonants straightforward. Stress is generally on the first syllable of the word (discounting any non-separable prefix: *geben* 'give'; *vergeben* 'forgive'; *ausgeben* 'spend').

German is noted for its aspirated pronunciation of consonants and the placement of glottal stops before initial vowels. In all positions single written <s> is voiced (to /z/; while <z> is pronounced /ts/). Conversely, <v> is devoiced (to /f/; <w> is pronounced voiced /v/), as are most final consonants (e.g. *Tod* 'death' is pronounced identically to *tot* 'dead'). In the north, final post-vocalic *-g* is pronounced as if *-ch* (thus *Tag* 'day' and *nach* 'after' rhyme, as do *Pfennig* 'penny' and *mich* 'me').

The standard language, insofar as one exists at all, is based on dialects which underwent the "Second Consonantal Sound Shift" in the late first millennium. This notably shifted /t/ to /(t)s/ and /p/ to /(p)f/, thus *Wasser* 'water' (Dutch *water*); *zehn* 'ten' (Dutch *tien*); *Pfeffer* 'pepper' (Dutch *peper*). German is generally pronounced (and <r> is trilled) farther forward in the mouth the farther south you go – giving Austrian and Bavarian German a markedly different sound from northern varieties (such as that of the Hanover region upon which the spoken language generally taught to foreigners is based; 13.2).

As with West Germanic languages in general, stressed syllables are strengthened and lengthened, although long vowels (often marked with a further <h> in modern German, e.g. *Zahn* 'tooth', *Lohn* 'wage') are also clearly distinguished from short.

13.2   Standard

The standardization of German was complex, but the outcome in terms of the written language is pleasingly regular. There remains no specific spoken standard – German newsreaders and announcers, for example, happily betray their geographical origins.

There are other varieties of High German in use which are clearly distinct from the language described as "German", but largely mutually intelligible with it.

Yiddish emerged in Central Europe in the ninth century as the language of the Ashkenazi Jews, based fundamentally on High German but containing elements of Hebrew and Aramaic, written in the Hebrew alphabet.

Luxembourgish is part of the Moselle-Franconian group of western Central German dialects, but now has its own written standard and has become the national language of Luxembourg.

Swiss German is the name given to a series of dialects spoken in Switzerland and Liechtenstein, the vast majority of which are part of the Alemannic group of southern Upper German and therefore quite distant from the variety on which the standard language is based. In speech, these are preferred to the standard language even in relatively formal settings, including in most broadcasting. However, formal writing continues to be in (Swiss) Standard German.

Given the lack of political unity in German-speaking lands until the mid 19th century, wide dialect variation across them was a constant feature throughout the Middle Ages and Early Modern era. Dialects were split into "Low" (northern) and "High" (southern), distinguished primarily by pronunciation of certain consonants. Luther's Bible translation, based on central German dialects but tending towards "High", formed the basis for what became a standard written form of "German". Over time, this "High" form took over from Low German across the north as the language of administration and education, and eventually in common use. As a result, there is now much less dialect variation in the north than in the south. Thus, even though they are geographically distant from the origin of the written standard, northern dialects are now regarded as the nearest to a "standard" spoken form.

German displays umlaut on low vowels to mark fronting (<ä>, <ö>, <ü>; thus <ä> and <e> are in fact pronounced alike), usually where a high vowel once followed (or still follows) a subsequent consonant (*England* 'England'; *Engländer* 'Englishman'); the distinction may now serve as a grammatical marker (*Mutter* 'mother', *Mütter* 'mothers'; *backen* 'bake', *Bäcker* 'baker'). German is also noted for the *scharfes S,* the <ß> character originally representing <sz> but now seen as a separate letter (except in Switzerland, where it is written *ss*).

German also marks all nouns with an initial capital letter, a practice which was once widespread in other Germanic languages, but which is now exclusive to German. German is also strict about separating clauses with commas: *ich sehe, dass er da ist* 'I see that he is there'.

Austria and Switzerland have their own written standards (and, as noted above, "Swiss German" is separate even from these).

Although orthographical standards are agreed across all three countries and the standard versions are mutually intelligible, they can exhibit some significant variation. Grammatically, there are different tendencies around forming the past with an auxiliary verb rather than a verb ending (and which auxiliary verb is used), and there can be notable differences in genders (particularly in new words to do with technology or popular culture). There are also marked differences in vocabulary, most obviously around food, and there is also some variation in the use of prefixes (particularly in Switzerland).

German underwent a minor spelling reform in the late 1990s, aimed at regularising certain points of orthography. Despite initial controversy, it is now widely accepted.

13.3 Vocabulary

Modern German vocabulary is largely of Germanic origin, and generally closer to older languages such as Old High German, Anglo-Saxon and Gothic (Chapter 4) than Modern English is. There was once significant resistance to borrowings, but in the modern language they are increasingly common, particularly from English.

Key numbers:

1 eins, 2 zwei, 3 drei, 4 vier, 5 fünf, 6 sechs, 7 sieben, 8 acht, 9 neun;
10 zehn, 11 elf, 12 zwölf, 13 dreizehn, 16 sechszehn, 17 siebzehn;
20 zwanzig, 24 vierundzwanzig, 100 hundert, 1000 tausend;
456789 vierhundertsechsundfünfzigtausendsiebenhundertneunundachtzig.

Zwei 'two' often appears as *zwo* in counting, or where otherwise necessary to distinguish clearly from *drei* 'three'.

Allowing for the Second Consonantal Sound Shift (13.1), this means that core German vocabulary is close to English and Dutch: *hier* 'here'; *das* 'that'; *haben* 'have'; *Apfel* 'apple'; *vergeben* 'forgive'.

Personal pronouns (masculine/feminine/neuter):

	Singular (1st, 2nd, 3rd)			Plural (1st, 2nd, 3rd)		
Nominative	*ich*	*du*	*er/sie/es*	*wir*	*ihr*	*sie*
Accusative	*mich*	*dich*	*ihn/sie/es*	*uns*	*euch*	*sie*
Genitive	*mein_*	*dein_*	*sein/ihr/sein_*	*unser_*	*eur_*	*ihr_*
Dative	*mir*	*dir*	*ihm/ihr/ihm*	*uns*	*euch*	*ihnen*

When standing alone, the genitive forms take the neuter ending *-es*.

The third person reflexive form, both accusative and dative, is *sich*.

In the modern language, *Sie* is the polite second person form. It behaves grammatically (whether the reference is singular or plural) as a third person plural (distinguished in writing by capitalization). Its use is declining, particularly in the south.

Interrogative pronouns:

- *wer* 'who'; *was* 'what'; *wann* 'when'; *wie* 'how'; *wo* 'where'.

Relative and demonstrative pronouns are similar to articles (13.4).

German is famed for its tendency to group nouns (and sometimes adjectives) together as a single word: *Geschwindigkeitsbegrenzung* 'speed limit', *Überwachungsverein* 'monitoring body', *kostenpflichtig* 'chargeable, at own cost', *autobahnähnlich* 'similar to a motorway'.

13.4   Grammar

Common plural forms for nouns:

- Masculine: *Wagen-Wagen* 'car(s)', *Apfel-Äpfel* 'apple(s)'; *Tag-Tage* 'day(s)', *Floh-Flöhe* 'flea(s)';
- Feminine: *Zeitung-Zeitungen* 'newspaper(s)';
- Neuter: *Haus-Häuser* 'house(s)', *Feld-Felder* 'field(s)'.

Dative plural adds *-n*: *Äpfeln, Tagen, Flöhen, Häusern, Feldern* etc.

There is also a set of "weak" nouns (*Held* 'hero', *Präsident* 'President'), all bar one masculine in the modern language, with the ending *-(e)n* in all cases except the nominative singular. Borrowings from English or French (*Auto* 'car', *Fan* 'fan') often form the plural in *-s* in all cases including the dative.

By the standards of Western European languages, the German noun is remarkably conservative and thus extraordinarily complex. It, or its supporting words, is marked for singular or plural (there are no fewer than seven common ways of doing this, plus many irregulars and dialectal variations), three genders and four cases. Cases are generally marked on preceding words but the dative plural almost always ends in *-n* (*mit den Flöhen* 'with the fleas'; *zu den Häusern* 'to the houses') and the genitive singular masculine and neuter in *-s* except for "weak" nouns (*des Apfels Kern* 'core of the apple'; *das Tor eines Feldes* 'the gate of a field'; *das Kennzeichen eines Helden* 'the mark of a hero'). However, the genitive is in marked decline in the modern language; it has already in effect merged with the dative with feminine nouns, and regardless of gender it is often replaced by workaround constructions using the dative in colloquial usage. The loss from nouns of the singular masculine and neuter dative ending *-e* is also nearly complete even in the written language, now restricted almost exclusively to set phrases (*zu Hause* 'at home [at the house]').

Verb endings (*lachen* 'laugh'; *singen* 'sing'),
1st, 2nd, 3rd person – singular; plural:
- weak, present: *lache, lachst, lacht; lachen, lacht, lachen;*
- strong, present: *singe, singst, singt; singen, singt, singen;*
- weak, past: *lachte, lachtest, lachte; lachten, lachtet, lachten;*
- strong, past: *sang, sangst, sang; sangen, sangt, sangen.*

Past participles are weak *gelacht,* strong *gesungen;* but note absence of *ge-* if there is already an inseparable prefix (*bestellt* 'ordered') or if infinitive ends *-ieren* (*studiert* 'studied'). Imperative is singular *lach/sing,* plural *lacht/singt,* polite *lachen Sie/singen Sie.*

With rare exceptions involving dummy subjects, all German main verbs must have a subject (unlike most Latin-derived languages).

Verbs are marked for present or past. "Weak" verbs mark the past by adding a dental suffix (typically <t>; *ich lache* 'I laugh', *ich lachte* 'I laughed'); as in English, irregular verbs are typically (but not always) "strong" and form their past instead by changing the root vowel (*ich singe* 'I sing', *ich sang* 'I sang'); with the exception of the third person singular, endings to agree with the subject are similar for both present and past. Some strong verbs also exhibit changes to the root vowel in the second and third person singular (*ich sehe* 'I see', *du siehst* 'you see'). Many speakers avoid the past form for all but the most common verbs, preferring to indicate the past with an auxiliary verb, usually *haben* 'have' or with verbs of motion *sein* 'be', plus the past participle (*du hast gelacht* 'you laughed'; *er hat gesungen* 'he sang'; *sie ist angekommen* 'she arrived'); the pluperfect uses relevant past forms of the auxiliary (*du hattest gelacht* 'you had laughed'; *sie war angekommen* 'she had arrived'). Some common verbs (typically, other than in the most formal language, only auxiliaries and modals including *sein* and *haben*) may also be directly marked for present conjunctive (*er sei, sie habe*), or past conjunctive (which generally doubles as a conditional form: *er wäre, sie hätte*). The conditional is otherwise formed with the past conjunctive form of *werden* plus infinitive (*wir würden darüber lachen* 'we would laugh about it'). The passive is formed with the relevant present/past form of *werden* plus past participle and preposition *von* (*dieses Lied wird gesungen* 'this song is sung'; *es wurde hier von den Römern gebaut* 'it was built here by the Romans'); this is possible even with a dummy subject (*es wird gelacht* 'there is laughing'; *auf den Straßen wurde gesungen* 'there was singing in the streets'). Other meanings (future, potential, obligation, etc) may be expressed through auxiliaries/modals plus infinitive (*sie werden lachen* 'they will laugh'; *du kannst gut singen* 'you can sing well'; *ich muss ihm vergeben* 'I must forgive him'). Notably some verbs (e.g. *vergeben*) take an object in the dative rather than the accusative case.

One peculiarity of the German verbal system is that the conjunctive mood may be used for "indirect speech", to indicate something is reported rather than known: *er habe gesungen* '(I was told that) he sang'; *sie sei schon angekommen* '(apparently) she already arrived'.

The article or another determiner is marked for case and (in the singular) gender; however, only masculine singular nouns mark a distinction between subject (nominative) and direct object (accusative).

Articles:

	Indefinite			Definite			
	Masc.	Fem.	Neuter	Masc.	Fem.	Neuter	Plural
Nominative	*ein*	*eine*	*ein*	*der*	*die*	*das*	*die*
Accusative	*einen*			*den*			
Genitive	*eines*	*einer*	*eines*	*des*	*der*	*des*	*der*
Dative	*einem*		*einem*	*dem*		*dem*	*den*

Relative pronouns generally take the same form as definite articles: *der Mann, den ich gesehen habe* 'The man (whom) I saw'; *die Frau, mit der ich gesprochen habe* 'The woman with whom I spoke'.

In the modern language, the only demonstrative pronoun is *dieser-diese-dieses* 'this, that', which declines in line with *der-die-das;* in formal use it may occasionally be joined by *jener-jene-jenes* 'that'. However, the articles themselves may serve a demonstrative purpose when stressed: *ja, den habe ich gesehen* 'yes, it is him [this one] I saw'; *das war zu der Zeit, als wir zusammen waren* 'that was at the (specific) time when we were together'.

Attributive adjectives have two sets of endings depending essentially on whether they need to mark case (*ein guter Mann* 'a good man') or if it is already apparent from an article or determiner (*der gute Mann* 'the good man'). Predicative adjectives are unmarked (*der Mann ist gut* 'the man is good'). Adverbs are also unmarked, as in most other Germanic languages (*sie hat es gut gesungen* 'she sang it well'; *wir haben laut gelacht* 'we laughed loudly').

Comparison requires the ending *-(e)r*, typically with umlaut, and the conjunction *als* (as this is a conjunction, both elements of the comparison remain in the same case): *er ist größer als ich* 'he is bigger than me [he is bigger than I (am)]'.

Pejorative is with determiner *wenig: er ist weniger groß als ich*. Equative is with *so ... wie* 'as ... as': *er ist so groß wie ich*. Superlative takes ending *-(e)st*, typically with umlaut: *das größte* 'the biggest', *am schönsten* '(at) the nicest', *vom feinsten* 'of the finest'.

Even in the formal written language, prepositions may merge with definite articles, particularly in the masculine/neuter: *in+dem=im; in+das=ins; zu+der=zur* etc. They govern the accusative, dative or (exceptionally, in formal writing) genitive case, or in some instances the accusative or dative depending on motion towards: *ich gehe ins Kino* 'I go into the cinema'; *ich bin im Kino* 'I am in the cinema'.

Key prepositions:
- with accusative: *für* 'for', *gegen* 'against', *um* 'around';
- with dative: *bei* 'with, by', *mit* 'with', *von* 'from, of', *zu* 'to';
- with either: *an* 'at, to', *auf* 'on(to)', *in* 'in(to)', *vor* 'before'.

Despite the potential flexibility provided by case marking, word order is strict and complex. German is fundamentally an SOV and V2 language. All elements of the verb phrase go to the end of the clause except the main verb, whose position varies – in interrogative clauses it goes first or second; in main clauses it goes second; otherwise it is final even after all other elements of the verb phrase (*hast du schon gesehen, ob er da war?* 'did you already see if he was there? [have-you-already-seen-whether-he-there-was]'; *gestern hast du darüber gelacht* 'yesterday you laughed about it [yesterday-have-you-about-it-laughed]'; *ich habe gehört, dass sie darüber lachen konnten* 'I heard that they were able to laugh about it [I-have-heard-that-they-about-it-to-laugh-were-able]'). This "verb-second" rule applies regardless of what comes first, even if it is another clause (*als du ihm vergeben hast, habt ihr darüber gelacht* 'when you forgave him, you laughed about it'). There are also separable verbs, similar to phrasal verbs in English except that in infinitive and participle forms the prepositional element goes first (*mitbringen* 'bring along [with-bring]'; *ich bringe meinen Bruder mit* 'I bring my brother along'; *ich habe meinen Bruder mitgebracht* 'I have brought my brother along'). There are also strict rules about the order of other phrases, including the positioning towards the end of the clause of the negative particle *nicht*, which is usually after the main verb but appears before it in subordinate clauses (*ich lache nicht darüber* 'I do not laugh about it'; *gestern habe ich gehört, dass wir nicht darüber lachen konnten* 'yesterday I heard that we were not able to laugh about it'). However, constructions with the negative determiner *kein* are preferred to those with *nicht* in many instances (*ich sang kein Lied* 'I did not sing a song [I-sang-no-song]').

Yes/no questions are by inversion (specifically to place verb first rather than second in the clause):

- *sie singt* 'she sings'; *singt sie?* 'does she sing?'

Answer *ja* 'yes', *nein* 'no'; *doch* 'yes [to a negative]'.

13.5   Character

German is a fundamentally noun-based language. Constructions which in other languages would be verb-focused are often based around noun phrases in German: *bei schlechtem Wetter, bleiben wir zu Hause* 'if the weather is bad [with bad weather], we will stay at home'.

The modern language can exhibit a preference for a remarkable degree of precision. Specific linguistic concepts such as *Ausbau* or philosophical concepts such as *Dasein* do not appear to hold their precise meaning in translation, and they are often simply carried over exactly as they are into other languages. There are numerous other terms, notably almost always nouns, which defy adequate translation: *Schadenfreude, Weltmüdigkeit, Gemütlichkeit*, etc.

Vater unser im Himmel, geheiligt werde dein Name; dein Reich komme; dein Wille geschehe; wie im Himmel so auf Erden. Unser tägliches Brot gib uns heute. Und vergib uns unsere Schuld, wie auch wir vergeben unsern Schuldigern; und führe uns nicht in Versuchung, sondern erlöse uns von dem Bösen.

14

DUTCH

Of Western Europe's major national languages, Dutch has by far the fewest native speakers (now numbering around 25 million). It is, however, a language with some global significance and it is a worthy topic for linguistic study in its own right, as a language close to German but one which has ended up with a much less conservative grammatical structure.

Derived from poorly attested Low Franconian dialects, Dutch is spoken across almost the whole of the Netherlands and the majority of Belgium (by population). Although they are not mutually intelligible, many Dutch speakers can understand written German to some degree. It is also noteworthy that many traditional dialects in northern Germany, known as "Low German", are closer (at least phonologically) to Standard Dutch than to Standard German (Chapter 13). Dutch also has the distinction, among national languages, of being the most closely related to English.

Dutch was also a colonial language, having been spoken in the past in all five continents. Although away from Europe it has now largely been displaced by local languages, creoles or English, it remains the official language of the South American country of Suriname and it is still spoken in parts of the Caribbean. It has also left a notable mark in Southern Africa in the form of what has become the distinct but still generally mutually intelligible Afrikaans (Chapter 15).

14.1 Phonology

Dutch shares with German a harsh sound, although somewhat less so because consonants are not pronounced with the same degree of aspiration. As a result of these frequent but soft consonants, modern Dutch can sound almost robotic to non-speakers.

The Dutch of the Netherlands is marked by the particularly strong (and long) pronunciation of /x/ (similar to Scottish 'lo<u>ch</u>'), written <g> or <ch>. This is a softer, shorter sound in Belgium, and it is therefore an obvious marker of the distinction between the spoken varieties in each country. Belgian Dutch is also characterized by a near devoicing of /v/.

The termination *-en* is common in written Dutch, including as a frequent grammatical suffix. However, in all but the most formal or careful speech, the /n/ in this ending is now barely pronounced.

Dutch also has a range of complex diphthongs which can cause confusion for learners whose native tongues do not include them. However, Dutch did not undergo the "Second Consonantal Sound Shift" (13.1), meaning that some words remain close to English: *appel* 'apple', *water* 'water', *dertien* 'thirteen', *wat is dat?* 'what is that?'

Dutch is pronounced well to the back of the mouth and, as with other West Germanic languages, stressed syllables are strengthened and lengthened. In the Netherlands there is a generally falling intonation; in Belgium this is more even, and often perceived as more melodic.

14.2 Standard

Initially, the standard language was based on the speech of Antwerp. However, the current standard is primarily based on educated usage in the Amsterdam area. It underwent a thorough revision in the late 1940s, and it is thus somewhat closer to the modern spoken language than that of most other major Western European languages.

The result retained a system whereby vowels pronounced alike may still be written single or double depending on whether they are in closed or open syllables: *naam* 'name', but *namen* 'names'.

However, the most noteworthy aspect of the recency of standardization is the abolition of grammatical case (except for some pronouns) and the general merger of the masculine and feminine gender. Unlike in German, Dutch nouns (and their surrounding words) are not marked for case except in archaic set phrases and some place names. This reflected changes which had already taken place in most Dutch dialects, but it does give the language a quite distinct flavour from German.

Written accents are not used as grammatical markers. However, acute accents may be used to mark emphasis (*een* 'a, an'; *één* 'one'); the diaresis may be used to mark separation at word boundaries in compound words: *drieëntwintig* 'twenty three [three-and-twenty]'. The digraph <ij> was once, but is no longer, considered a separate letter.

The current standard was adopted in both the Netherlands (as well as Suriname) and Belgium at much the same time. Therefore, the Dutch of both countries (often referred to as *Hollands* in the Netherlands and *Vlaams* in Belgium) is identical in formal settings, with some very minor variations in grammar, vocabulary and spelling preference.

14.3   Vocabulary

Dutch vocabulary is overwhelmingly of Germanic origin, although Dutch lacked the same purism as German through the 19th century and has generally allowed more borrowings, notably from French.

Key numbers:
1 een, 2 twee, 3 drie, 4 vier, 5 vijf, 6 zes, 7 zeven, 8 acht, 9 negen;
10 tien, 11 elf, 12 twaalf, 15 vijftien, 16 zestien, 17 zeventien;
20 twintig, 24 vierentwintig; 100 honderd; 1000 duizend;
456789 vierhonderd zesenvijftigduizend zevenhonderd negenentachtig.

One markedly irregular number has developed: *tachtig* 'eighty'.

Because of sound changes which occurred in southern (High) German dialects but not farther north and west (14.1), Dutch vocabulary is often more recognizably close to English than Standard German is. However, some key word classes (notably pronouns) have undergone further changes to become quite distinct from either German or English.

Personal pronouns forms (masculine/feminine/impersonal):

	Singular (1st, 2nd, 3rd)			Plural (1st, 2nd, 3rd)		
Sg. full	*ik*	*jij*	*hij/zij/het*	*wij*	*jullie*	*zij*
Sg. reduced	*'k*	*je*	*ie/ze/'t*	*we*		*ze*
Pl. full	*mij*	*jou*	*hem/haar/het*	*ons*	*jullie*	*hen, hun*
Pl. reduced	*me*	*je*	*'m/d'r/'t*			*ze*
Possessive	*mijn*	*jouw*	*zijn/haar*	*onze*	*jullie*	*hun*

Reduced forms are usually used as subjects or after prepositions. With the exceptions of *je* and *ze,* they are not generally used in writing (except when representing speech).

The polite second person form (singular or plural *u* in all cases, possessive *uw*) is maintained in Belgium but appears to be falling out of use in the Netherlands. In southern dialects, including in Belgium, the second person form *gij (ge)* may be preferred to *jij (je)*.

Generally, reference back to common gender nouns is by *hij* or *hem* (possessive *zijn*) except if they are naturally feminine, although in very formal contexts an original feminine gender of the noun (if known) may be applied (*haar*). A recent development is that *haar* is occasionally heard in speech as the possessive with reference to neuter nouns, but *zijn* is still considered standard.

Dutch does usually retain, in the third person plural, a distinction between direct object *hen* and indirect object *hun* (however, this distinction is contested by some historical grammarians and, in spoken Dutch, either may be replaced by *ze* if referring to people).

All forms of the demonstrative are *deze* 'this, these' and *die* 'that, those' except the neuter singular, which is *dit* and *dat* respectively; *die* is also used as the relative pronoun (or *dat* with reference to a neuter singular), alongside personal *wie* and impersonal *waar*.

Common interrogatives are *wie* 'who' (possessive *wiens* 'whose'), *wat* 'what', *waar* 'where', *wanneer* 'when' and *hoe* 'how'.

Dutch has its fair share of long words (themselves usually combinations of other words), but they are marginally rarer than in German – in writing, hyphens are more often employed: *Noord-Duitsland* (German *Norddeutschland)* 'Northern Germany'.

14.4 Grammar

Nouns in Dutch can be one of two genders, common ("*de*-words") or neuter ("*het*-words"). Plurals are typically formed with the addition of the ending *-(e)n* or *-s* (written *-'s* after vowels); there is no easy way of determining which, but there are some patterns.

Verbs are marked for present or past (which adds *-t-* or *-d-* before the ending). Generally, plural verbs have a single ending *-en*; singular have *-t* in the present (except the first person, which has no ending) and *-e* in the past. With some common verbs second and third person singular forms are still distinct from each other. Other tenses are formed with auxiliaries plus either the infinitive (ending *-en*) or the past participle (typically with prefix *ge-* and ending *-t* or *-d* for weak verbs or *-en* for strong): *ik zou dansen* 'I would dance'; *jij hebt gedanst* 'you have danced'; *jij hebt gezongen* 'you have sung'; *zij had gedanst* 'she had danced'; *wij zouden hebben gedanst* 'we would have danced'. Progressive aspect can be indicated by use of a verbal noun (in effect the infinitive) after *aan het* 'at the', appearing at the end of the clause: *zij zijn gewoon liedjes <u>aan het zingen</u>* 'they are just singing songs'. The subjunctive/conjunctive is now rarely encountered in Dutch, with its use (expressing command or desire) now restricted to set phrases.

Typical verb endings:

Weak verb *maken* 'make' – 1st, 2nd, 3rd person singular; plural:
- present *ik maak, jij maakt, hij/het maakt; wij/jullie/zij maken*;
- past *ik/jij/hij/het maakte; wij/jullie/zij maakten.*

Strong verb *zingen* 'sing' – 1st, 2nd, 3rd person singular; plural:
- present *ik zing, jij zingt, hij/het zingt; wij/jullie/zij zingen*;
- past *ik/jij/hij/het zong; wij/jullie/zij zongen.*

Past participles generally take the prefix *ge-* (*gemaakt* 'made'; *gezongen* 'sung'; *gestudeerd* 'studied'), but this is dropped when the verb already contains an inseparable prefix (*besteld* 'ordered').

In the present tense, the final *-t* is generally omitted in the second (but not third) person in case of inversion: *maak jij* but *maakt hij*; this unmarked form (*maak, zing,* etc) doubles as the imperative.

The definite article is *de* (plural and common singular) or *het* (neuter singular). The indefinite article is invariable *een*; however, adjectives behave differently after it depending on gender, as they do not take the otherwise usual attributive *-e* ending with a neuter singular noun: *de grote hond* 'the big dog'; *een grote hond* 'a big dog'; *het grote huis* 'the big house'; but *een groot huis* 'a big house' (this is called the strong declension and also applies after other determiners, e.g. *geen* 'no', *elk* 'each': *geluk heeft geen groot huis nodig* 'happiness does not require a big house'). As in most other Germanic languages, adverbs are unmarked, as are adjectives used predicatively: *ik heb vrijwillig gedanst* 'I danced voluntarily'; *dat was vrijwilling* 'that was voluntary'; *de hond is groot* 'the dog is big'.

Key prepositions:
*   *van* 'of, from', *met* 'with', *naar* 'to', *in* 'in', *op* 'on', *bij* 'at'.

Word order is complex. Fundamentally, Dutch is V2; in main clauses, the main verb is placed second regardless of the first element, and the main verb is first or second in interrogative clauses; all verbs and participles are otherwise final, including in subordinate clauses (although typically in Dutch, unlike German, the main verb precedes any participles or infinitives even in subordinate clauses where they are all placed finally): *vandaag doe ik dat* 'I'm doing that today [Today-do-I-that]'; *doe je dat vandaag?* 'Are you doing that today?'; *ik weet zeker dat ik dat vandaag doe* 'I know for sure that I am doing that today [I-know-certainly-that-I-that-today-do]', *ik weet zeker dat ik dat vandaag heb gedaan* 'I know for sure that I have done that today'. There are separable verbs, which as in German see the initial component detached (and moved to the end in main and interrogative clauses): _meebrengen_ 'bring along'; _ik breng mijn broer mee_ 'I bring by brother along'; _ik heb mijn broer meegebracht_ 'I brought my brother along'; _breng ik mijn broer mee?_ 'do I bring my brother along?' The negative particle is _niet,_ usually placed towards the end of the clause and always after the main verb (except in subordinate clauses, where it precedes it): _ik doe dit thuis niet_ 'I don't do this at home'; _het is te hopen dat ik dit thuis niet doe_ 'It is hoped that I do not do this at home'. The negative article _geen_ is often preferred: _ik spreek geen Engels_ 'I do not speak English [I-speak-no-English]'; _ik heb geen hond meer_ 'I no longer have a dog [I-have-no-dog-more]'.

Yes/no questions are by inversion:

- _zij zingt_ 'she sings'; _zingt zij?_ 'does she sing?'

Answer _ja_ 'yes'; _nee_ 'no'.

14.5   Character

Like German, Dutch is a largely noun-focused language. The prime difference is that Dutch is similar in structure to what German would have become, had its standard not maintained such a conservative grammatical form.

Dutch is also notable for its proliferation of diminutive forms, typically ending _-je_ (also _-ske_ in Belgium) often with other modifications to aid pronunciation, indicating small size or endearment: _zusje_ 'little sister'; _appeltje_ '(little) apple'; _filmpje_ 'movie, picture'; _dingetje_ 'little thing, thingy'. Some have now developed independent meanings: _meisje_ 'girl [little maid]', _ijsje_ 'ice cream [little ice]'.

Onze vader die in de Hemel zijt, Uw naam worde geheiligd, Uw rijk kome, Uw wil gescheide op aarde zoals in de Hemel. Geef ons heden ons dagelijks brood en vergeef ons onze schulden, zoals ook wij vergeven aan onze schuldenaren. En leid ons niet in bekoring, maar verlos ons van het kwade.

15

AFRIKAANS

The inclusion of Afrikaans in this book is, of course, cheating somewhat because the language is profoundly not European – as is in evidence from its very name. However, it is a unique example of how a Western European and Germanic language developed when it became intercontinental but then had only a limited connection to its original homeland. This extraordinary linguistic phenomenon therefore provides a clear view of what could have happened to other languages had the process of language change (with all the phonological development and grammatical regularization that entails) not been slowed down by the pressure to conform to a "standard" variety.

Alongside English, Dutch (from which Afrikaans is derived; Chapter 14) remained the official language of South Africa until 1925. Afrikaans was added as an official language that year, and it took over fully from Dutch in subsequent decades, remaining official (and in practice one of two main languages of administration) through the transition to democracy towards the end of the 20th century. Furthermore, it was spoken in a country in which television was not introduced until the 1970s. It therefore provides an example of how an official national language looks having been standardized centuries after many of the national languages of Western Europe.

Afrikaans remains the first language of a significant share of the population of South Africa and Namibia, particularly away from the east coast, and is widely understood by much of the entire population.

A further socio-linguistic curiosity is that in Southern Africa conversations can be held by two speakers each using their own native language – it is not unusual, therefore, to hear one person in a conversation speaking English and the other Afrikaans.

15.1   Phonology

Despite many obvious similarities, it is immediately evident even to the untrained ear that Afrikaans is clearly not Dutch. It retains a certain harshness, but rather less so than some other Germanic languages. This is in part because it has dropped some final consonants and consonant clusters, but it has added (or maintained) broken diphthong-like sounds in words such as *see* 'sea'.

It remains, nevertheless, clearly derived from Dutch (14.1) and thus many of the fundamental sounds (and, helpfully for potential learners, phonological similarities with English) are the same. As with Dutch, the location of articulation is back in the mouth and stressed syllables are both strengthened and lengthened.

15.2   Standard

Afrikaans was standardized in the 1920s, which is remarkably late compared to the national languages of Western Europe, although before the most recent reforms of Dutch. In the past century, therefore, both Afrikaans and Dutch have moved away from what was in effect the previous common standard (albeit the former much more so).

Afrikaans simplified its spelling system, most notably (versus Dutch) by amending or removing some letters and combinations, including:
- <ij> to <y>, but -*lijk* to -*lik* (*vyf* 'five', *lelik* 'ugly');
- <ou(w)> and <au(w)> to <ou> (*jou* 'your', *dou* 'dew');
- <z>, <s> merged to <s> (*see* 'sea', *plesier* 'pleasure');
- <ch>, <g> merged to <g>, but *sch-* to *sk-* (*agt* 'eight', *skip* 'ship');
- medial <g> omitted (*reën* 'rain', *môre* 'morning', *sê* 'say'); and
- medial <v> to <w> (*sewe* 'seven'), or omitted (*aand* 'evening').

Afrikaans also removed some final letters, notably final -*n* after a vowel, and also final -*t* (occasionally with other modifications) where it is not clearly pronounced; this works well for phonemic representation (for example *sewe* 'seven' reflects pronunciation not just in Afrikaans but also in some Dutch dialects more accurately than Dutch *zeven*), but does lead to some confusion when the letter reappears apparently irregularly in grammatically derived forms (e.g. *sewentien* 'seventeen', and also many plurals and adjectival endings). The loss of -*n* and -*t* from the spoken language in many instances therefore also had profound grammatical implications, notably concerning the formation of the plural and verbal inflection (15.4).

Although they are relatively rare in practice, theoretically all vowels in Afrikaans can take an acute accent (*é*), a diaresis (*ë*) or a circumflex (*ê*). These are designed to aid pronunciation but are in fact commonly used for emphasis or distinction (e.g. *dié* 'this/that' versus *die* 'the'; *sê* 'say' versus possessive particle *se*).

One marked peculiarity of Afrikaans writing is the initial apostrophe, notably for the indefinite article *'n*. This sees the letter immediately after the apostrophe written lower case even if it is at the start of the sentence, in which case the initial letter of the following word takes the capitalization: *'n Appel het ek geëet* '(It's) an apple (that) I ate'.

15.3   Vocabulary

Afrikaans vocabulary is overwhelmingly shared with Dutch, with additional items to cover the natural progression of the language in a new setting (in much the same way as English developed to describe new things its speakers encountered in the American Wild West or the Australian Outback).

Key numbers:
1 een, 2 twee, 3 drie, 4 vier, 5 vyf, 6 ses, 7 sewe, 8 agt, 9 nege;
10 tien, 11 elf, 12 twaalf, 16 sestien, 17 sewentien, 19 negentien;
20 twintig, 24 vier-en-twintig; 100 eenhonderd; 100 eenduisend;
456789 vierhonderd ses-en-vyftig duisend sewehonderd nege-en-tagtig.

As well as significant borrowings from English and French, there is some additional vocabulary taken from neighbouring Khoi and Bantu languages, Portuguese and perhaps most curiously Malay (including core vocabulary items such as *amper* 'almost'; *baie* 'very, much').

Personal pronouns (masculine/feminine/impersonal):

	Singular (1st, 2nd, 3rd)			Plural (1st, 2nd, 3rd)		
Subject	*ek*	*jy*	*hy/sy/dit*	*ons*	*julle*	*hulle*
Object	*my*	*jou*	*hom/haar/dit*			

The polite 'you' form, singular or plural, is *u* in all cases.

Informal Afrikaans does also allow some reduced forms (as in Dutch, though less commonly), most notably *'k (ek)* and *'t (dit)*.

Afrikaans has a specific possessive particle *se* (*die hond se huis* 'the dog's house'). Pronouns typically have their own possessive adjective forms, but these too are notable because with the sole exception of *sy* 'his' (versus *hom* 'him, himself') they all take the same form as the object personal pronoun (which also doubles as the reflexive pronoun): *my* 'me, my, myself', *hulle* 'they, them, their, themselves'. For possessive use, impersonal *dit* tends to be used alongside the possessive particle: *dit se* 'its'.

Dit is also merged, in all registers, with *is* 'is' to form *dis* 'it's'.

The emphasized invariable definite article *dié* is also used as the demonstrative pronoun, but it may be combined to indicate grade: *hier* 'here', *hierdie* 'this, these'; *daar* 'there', *daardie* 'that, those'.

The relative pronoun is always *wat* except after a preposition, when the interrogatives *wie* (for a person) or *waar* (for an object or idea) are substituted. This gives interrogative pronouns *wie* 'who', *wat* 'what' (also *watter* 'which') and *waar* 'where', alongside *wanneer* 'when' and *hoe* 'how'. Some of these may also be combined with a combination of *se* and *'n* (which gives *s'n*: *wie s'n* 'whose').

15.4 Grammar

As in English, nouns in Afrikaans no longer display inherent grammatical gender at all. The most common plural marker is the ending -e (*hond-honde* 'dog-dogs'; *huis-huise* 'house-houses') with relevant consonant doubling (*kop-koppe* 'head-heads'); any final -g in the singular is generally removed in the plural (*dag-dae* 'day-days'). Another common plural ending, notably for family terms or borrowings from English, is -s (*dogter-dogters* 'daughter-daughters'). There are also some notable irregular forms (*kind-kinders* 'child-children'). Typically, the -e plural matches -(e)n in Standard Dutch (14.4) and -s matches -s, but this is far from universal.

Verb forms (present-past):
- auxiliary *wees* 'be', *is-was*; *hê* 'have', *het-had (het gehad)*;
- modals *kan-kon; wil-wou; moet-moes; sal-sou.*

Active usage:
- *ek sing* 'I sing'; *ek bestel* 'I order';
- *ek het gesing* 'I sang, I have sung'; *ek het bestel* 'I ordered';
- *ek sal sing* 'I will sing'; *ek sal bestel* 'I will order';
- *ek sou sing* 'I would have sung'.

Modal usage (modals may be combined):
- *ek kan sing* 'I can sing'; *ek kan bestel* 'I can order';
- *ek kon sing* 'I used to be able to sing [but can no longer]';
- *ek kon gesing het* 'I could have sung';
- *ek moet bestel* 'I have to order';
- *ek moes bestel* 'I had to order';
- *dit sou kon gebeur het* 'that could have happened'.

Passive usage:
- *dit word gesing* 'it is (being) sung';
- *dis [dit is] gesing* 'it has been (being) sung';
- *dit was gesing* 'it was sung [but is no longer]';
- *dit sal gesing word* 'it will be sung'.

The pluperfect has largely fallen out of use in the modern language.

Verbs in Afrikaans are perhaps the most remarkably reduced element of the language. Only the auxiliary/modal verbs have distinct present and past forms. Other verbs, which are all entirely regular, have no more than two forms in common use – a base form (*sê* 'say', *werk* 'work', *sing* 'sing') and a past participle formed with the prefix *ge-* (*gesê, gewerk, gesing*); in fact, those with an existing inseparable prefix have only one form (e.g. *bestel* 'order', past participle also *bestel*). The base form standing alone marks the present tense in all persons, singular and plural (*sy sê* 'she says', *hulle werk* 'they work', *die honde sien* 'the dogs see'); it can also be used as an imperative (*sing!* 'sing!'). Additional meaning, including tense and voice, may be conveyed by combination of modals (including *sal* to indicate future) with the base form, or of other auxiliaries (including *word*, which has no past form of its own in the modern language, for the present passive) with the past participle. As in Dutch and almost all Western European languages, *gaan* 'go' has developed as an auxiliary to mark the near future alongside the base form (*ons gaan bestel* 'we are going to order'; *die honde gaan my sien* 'the dogs are going to see me'). Technically, the simplification of verb endings means Afrikaans is unique among Germanic languages in no longer distinguishing between "weak" and "strong" verbs; however, several common verbs still show vestiges of the "strong" past participle by retaining the ending *-n* even in the base form (*gaan* 'go', *sien* 'see', *doen* 'do').

The articles are invariable – definite *die* and indefinite *'n*; the latter is now pronounced as a schwa sound (i.e. as a neutral vowel, not unlike its usual English equivalent 'a' when unstressed). Adverbs are generally not marked, but most adjectives add an ending when appearing attributively (before a noun); the ending is almost always required for single-syllable adjectives and occasionally for others, and is typically *-e*, with further modifications required with some common adjectives (often removal of preceding consonant, *koud-koue* 'cold', *laag-lae* 'low'; or re-insertion of a letter where it once existed in the original Dutch form, *sleg-slegte* 'bad') and some outright irregular forms (*oud-ou* 'old'; thus *die hond is oud* 'the dog is old' but *dis die ou hond* 'it's the old dog').

Key prepositions:
- *van* 'of', *met* 'with', *vir* 'to, for', *in* 'in', *deur* 'by', *by* 'at'.

Word order is essentially as in Dutch – V2 in main clauses (thus the verb always appears as second element) and SOV in subordinate (*gister het ek die ou hond gesien, terwyl ek in die koue huis was* 'I saw the old dog yesterday when I was in the cold house [yesterday-have-I-the-old-dog-seen-when-I-in-the-cold-house-was]'). Separable verbs are used similarly to Dutch and German (*saambring* 'bring along'; *ek bring my broer saam* 'I bring my brother along'; *ek het my broer saamgebring* 'I brought my brother along').

Negation is a peculiarity, typically involving the placement of the particle *nie* towards the end of the clause after the main verb (except in subordinate clauses where it precedes it) but with repetition of *nie* as the final element if it is not already final, making double negation effectively compulsory in such instances (*ek het die ou hond <u>nie</u> gesien <u>nie</u>* 'I did not see the old dog [I-have-the-old-dog-not-seen-not]'); this final placement also applies after the negative article *geen* 'no' (*ek het <u>geen</u> honde gesien <u>nie</u>* 'I did not see any dogs'), as well as after the negative imperative particle *moenie* (*<u>moenie</u> in die koue huis sing <u>nie</u>* 'do not sing in the cold house'). The origin of this feature is unclear, and it continues to be debated among linguists.

Yes/no questions are by inversion:
- *sy sing* 'she sings'; *sing sy?* 'does she sing?'

Answer *ja* 'yes'; *nee* 'no'.

15.5   Character

Some language learners with an interest in Germanic languages, and particularly in Dutch, ask whether it is worth learning Afrikaans first. However, despite the obvious similarities, using Afrikaans as a "staging post" in this way is not recommended; it needs to be considered on its own merits.

Afrikaans broadly retains the character of Dutch, but arguably in a more exotic way given the different and various influences on it in recent centuries. It remains primarily noun-focused but, as is to be expected of a language standardized so late in time, it is structurally and phonologically considerably less conservative.

Studies in mutual intelligibility between Dutch and Afrikaans are often aligned with those looking at mutual intelligibility among Scandinavian languages (Chapter 12). Despite the language's original basis on the vernacular mainly of people from South Holland, Afrikaans speakers do generally report than they understand Belgian Dutch (or *Vlaams* 'Flemish') better than that of the Netherlands. Nevertheless, despite their linguistic proximity, Dutch and Afrikaans speakers coming together will often end up simply switching to English.

The broad phonological and grammatical structure of Afrikaans is undeniably considerably less complex than that of other Germanic and indeed Western European languages. However, this regularization should not be mistaken for simplicity; Afrikaans is as capable as any other language of expressing a wide range of nuances and complexities. Proficiency in it ultimately requires significant effort, just as it does with any other language.

Ons Vader wat in die hemele is, laat U Naam geheilig word. Laat U koninkryk kom. Laat U wil geskied, soos in die hemel net so ook op die aarde. Gee ons vandag ons daaglikse brood. En vergeef ons ons skulde, soos ons ook ons skuldenaars vergewe. En lei ons nie in versoeking nie, maar verlos ons van die Bose.

16

GERMANIC LANGUAGES

Our first clear view of a Germanic language (Gothic; Chapter 4) is from a text written fully four centuries after the Golden Age of Latin literature; in fact, the first attestation of an extant Germanic language (Old English) is from over a millennium after the earliest attestation of Latin. Perhaps primarily for this reason, Germanic languages have traditionally lacked the prestige of their Latin-derived cousins.

For all that, collectively, Germanic languages are spoken roughly as widely in both Western Europe and across the world as Latin-derived languages. By global standards, the two families are similar in many ways (sharing ultimately the same Indo-European ancestor and notable subsequent mutual influence), but profoundly different in others.

Phonologically, Germanic languages tend to be less vocalic, and therefore more reliant on hard consonantal sounds than Latin-derived languages. They can therefore sound rather harsher, particularly than French or Italian. Generally, though not always, they are pronounced farther back in the mouth; West Germanic languages also invariably show a distinct "stress timed" pattern which has the effect of both strengthening and lengthening stressed syllables.

Generally, Germanic languages retain a distinct neuter gender, although many in contemporary standard form do not distinguish masculine from feminine grammatically aside from in pronouns. The most noteworthy distinction from Latin-derived languages, however, is perhaps the more restrictive verb, which is marked directly for only two tenses, and which displays much more limited if any use of a subjunctive mood. Separable verbs are also a Germanic innovation.

In terms of vocabulary, Germanic languages tend towards building single words, whereas Latin-derived languages tend towards noun phrases. Borrowings from Latin-derived languages (particularly Latin and French) are more common across all Germanic languages, however, than the reverse.

One additional point of note regarding vocabulary is that, when expressing motion, Germanic languages tend to focus on the type of movement with a preposition added as part of the verb phrase to specify direction where required ('go over', 'walk in', 'run up'); Latinate languages tend more towards using verbs which specify the direction of movement intrinsically (e.g. Italian *entrare* 'go/walk/run in', Portuguese *salir* 'go/walk/run out', Spanish *subir* 'go/walk/run up', French *descendre* 'go/walk/run down').

During the second half of the second millennium Germanic languages came to be more common in science (including linguistics itself), but less so in music. Debate rages about whether this is a cause or a consequence of their basic character.

Insular Nordic languages were omitted from this handbook, as they have very few speakers globally. Nevertheless, they are fascinating because of their conservative nature (unlike Scandinavian languages, Icelandic still has verb endings for person and noun/adjective markers for four cases and three genders, as well as retaining two distinct older letters in its alphabet). As the focus was on learning languages rather than merely describing them, Modern English itself has not been covered either, despite its notable exceptionalism as a West Germanic language which has become something of a hybrid given significant influence from Norse, Latin and (Norman) French. Nevertheless, the information in this handbook should provide a platform for further Germanic linguistic study for those who need or wish to pursue it, including of Germanic languages as they developed away from Europe.

17

NEXT STEPS

This reference guide has presented an outline of every language relevant to understanding and being understood across the whole of Western Europe, and thus across much of the world.

The contention in this handlook is that language learning is more efficient and indeed more interesting if it is based on a platform which ties a knowledge of the core vocabulary together with an overall historical overview and a basic phonological and grammatical outline. If the objective is to learn a single language, an understanding of where it and any related languages (both in space and time) came from provides a window not just to linguistic but also to social and cultural history, which only serves to make the language learning journey more fascinating. Even more notably, however, this platform of vocabulary, history, phonology and grammar, available here for each language in just a few pages, gives us a clear foundation from which to acquire knowledge of several foreign languages without having to learn each from scratch.

With the platform in place, what are the next steps?

17.1   Motivation

The immediate next step is to be clear about what the purpose of learning any given language (or languages) is. Without clear purpose

---

and thus clear motivation, it is too easy to give up. The idea of fluency in another language sounds nice, but it does take effort. Any effort is most likely to succeed with a clear objective in mind. For example, if we are learning Italian just because we are attending a wedding in Italy next year, it is best to keep it light and limited and by all means simply use a phrasebook in conjunction with this handbook a guide; on the other hand, if we are learning Italian because we intend to move there, then fluency is the objective and we will want to go through all the various stages below to attain it.

17.2   Comprehensible Input

The next step is to find ways of receiving "comprehensible input". It is a universal truth that the more we read and, particularly, listen to a language (ideally both at the same time), the better we will get at it. Even without noticing immediately, we will inevitably begin to pick up its patterns, its wider vocabulary, the key points of its pronunciation and its core grammar. Not only can we make rapid progress in this way, but it has never been easier to have fun doing it – we now have access to a vast array of programmes and books, even simply on a tablet, from which we can choose what to watch, what to listen to and what to read. Since we are going to choose content in which we are naturally interested anyway, the process will inevitably be enjoyable.

17.3   Levels

It is important not to stay at "beginner" level forever. We must not let perfection get in the way of the good!

At each stage of the language learning process, all we need is a basic outline (such as that presented in this handbook); we do not need to understand absolutely every item of technical grammar or detailed phonetics before we move up a level. Remember, having given ourselves the platform provided by this book and then focused on "comprehensible input", we can (and should) move up levels quickly.

17.4   Speaking

It is not necessary to speak until we have moved up a few levels, but it is important to do so eventually. Speaking enables us to learn not just the phonology but also the patterns in our mouth to produce common sounds, words and phrases by mimicking and practice. In this way, a little like learning the words to a song becomes easier when we fit them to a tune, we should find we make further rapid progress.

Ideally, we will be able to create opportunities to chat to native speakers of the target language, but even without this we should use any free moment at all to practise. Driving alone? Try to describe the view from the car in the target language. Doing some exercises? Count down the seconds in the target language. Mowing the lawn? Try to assess a favourite sports team's season so far in the target language.

While it does depend a little on what our objectives and motivations are, typically listening and speaking will take priority over reading and writing. Language is, fundamentally, a spoken construct. After all, we learn our own native language by listening and speaking and only get to reading and writing later, and there is rarely any reason to do this in reverse when learning another language.

17.5   Review

Remember, the prime objective is creating understanding, not achieving perfection. By following these steps – establishing the platform, checking the motivation, focusing on the comprehensible input, moving up the levels and then using every opportunity to practise speaking, we will soon identify the gaps in grammar and particularly vocabulary which specifically matter to us; but we will also be well equipped to fill in these gaps – and to have fun doing it.

Learning languages is a proactive and, most of all, fun activity. Now just go and enjoy the challenge!

APPENDIX A

—

GLOSSARY

A.1 Glossary of terms

Ablative   a **case** usually marking 'by' or 'with'.

Accusative   a **case** usually marking an **object** (also used to indicate motion towards).

Active   a **clause** in which the subject is responsible for the action or feeling expressed [the boy throws the ball]. Opposite of **passive.**

Adjective   a word which "describes" or determines a **noun** [a blue ball].

Adverb   a word used to "describe" a verb [he threw it quickly] or to intensify an **adjective** [very big].

Animate   referring to a person (and often in practice also household pets or other family animals).

Article   a word specifying whether a **noun** is **definite** [the, la] or **indefinite** [a, an].

Aspect(ual)   the marking of a word (or phrase) to establish whether the action is complete or incomplete (can also mark progressive or habitual).

Attributive   said of an **adjective** appearing directly alongside the noun it supports (typically before in **Germanic** languages, but often after in others).

Auxiliary verb   a **verb** used with another verb or participle to make grammatical distinctions [it has happened, she must go, did you see?].

Base form	the unmodified form of a verb [sing, like]; in practice, the root word without any grammatical marker; see also **citation form**.
Case	the form of a **noun/pronoun** which shows its grammatical relationship to other words within the **clause**; cases include the **nominative**, objective/**accusative** and **possessive/genitive**.
Citation form	the unmodified form of a word (as it appears in the dictionary).
Clause	a grammatical unit in which words are put together to make sense; types include **main, interrogative** and **subordinate**.
Common	a grammatical **gender** combining masculine and feminine.
Comparative	a form of **adjective/adverb** which shows comparison to another element (usually a **noun/pronoun**) in the clause [bigger, more intelligent].
Complement	an element in the **clause** which completes what is said about the **subject** [she goes to Belfast, he is a teacher].
Compound	a word or phrase composed of two separate words placed together [computer game, *Schadenfreude*].
Conditional	a clause or verb form which indicates condition or hypothesis [if you bounced the ball she would come in]; also considered "**future** in the **past**".
Conjunction	a word connecting words or **clauses** [and, but, or, although]. Conjunctions may be coordinating or **subordinating**.
Conjunctive	in general, related to a **conjunction**; however, used in or with reference to **Germanic** languages, this often refers to a **mood,** typically similar to the **subjunctive** or the **conditional**.
Consonant	a speech sound or letter that is not a **vowel**.
Copula(tive)	a **verb** used to link elements of a clause [be, seem, become, appear].

Correlative	a word separated from another word in the sentence, but which goes together with it to form a single function. (both... and, *tio... kion*).
Dative	a **case**, typically marking an indirect **object**.
Definite	a specific, identifiable entity (usually already mentioned in the text), usually introduced in English by the **article** 'the'.
Demonstrative	a form which distinguishes a word from others which are the same **part of speech** [those, which].
Determiner	a word or phrase which is placed before a **noun** to express a number or quantity [some, many].
Diphthong	a sound arising from the pronunciation of two **vowels** in a single **syllable**.
Equative	**comparative** form expressing equal (rather than more or less than).
Future	a **tense** used to express actions or feelings which will occur in the future.
Gender	grouping of words into masculine, feminine or neuter classes (see also **common**), which may be either natural or purely grammatical.
Genitive	a **case**, aligned with the **possessive**.
Germanic	family of languages to which English belongs, alongside German, Dutch, the Scandinavian languages and others, all deriving from a single common ancestor later than Proto-Indo-European. Taken together, they are marked out grammatically by the use of **auxiliary verbs** to indicate **tense**, formation of verb forms and participles by changing the root **vowel**, and commonalities in **word order** as well as phonetics and vocabulary.
Gerund	the **noun** form of a **verb** [the postponing of the fixture].
Gerundive	the **adjective** form of a **verb**.
Gradation	degrees of gradation are used to indicate distance from the speaker and/or listener (this vs. that).

Imperative	a verb form (**mood**) introducing a command [go!]
Imperfect	see **perfect**.
Indefinite	opposite of **definite**, introduced in the **singular** in English by the article 'a'/'an'.
Infinitive	a basic **verb** form which is not coded for **person**.
Interrogative	a **clause**, **particle**, **verb** form or **adjective/pronoun** used for questions [Where would he find it? How did they do it?]
Italic	family of languages, the contemporary varieties of which derive from a common ancestor, Latin. Taken together, they are marked by their wide range of **verb suffixes**, distinct **word order** in the case of personal pronouns, and commonalities in pronunciation and vocabulary.
Latin(ate)	associated with or derived from Latin; see **Italic**.
Main clause	a **clause** which does not depend on any other clause in the sentence, also known as "independent"; opposite of **subordinate** and separate from **interrogative**.
Main verb	a **verb** expressing an action, event, state of feeling which is not a **participle** or **infinitive**.
Mood	a **verb** form expressing mood – typically now indicative, **subjunctive** or **imperative**.
Negation	grammatical form used to express that which is not the case, using **participles, prefixes, suffixes** or **correlatives** [un-, not, -n't, never].
Negative	see **negation**.
Nominative	a **case** used to indicate subject of the clause.
Noun	a "naming" word (of a thing, action or notion) [table, farm, happiness, vehicle].
Noun phrase	a phrase with a **noun** as its main point [the boy in the coat].
Object	an element in the **clause** to which the action or feeling in the clause happens, or which happens as a result of the action in the clause [the boy throws her the ball, we saw the moon, they gave it to him].

Objective	**case** marking an **object**, see **accusative**.
Part of speech	a set of words displaying the same grammatical property (e.g. **adjective, adverb, noun, particle, verb**), also known as "word class".
Participle	a word derived from a **verb** which may be used to change **tense** or **voice**, but which is also used as an **adjective**; in English there are two [e.g. from 'like': liked, liking].
Particle	a word with a grammatical function which does not change [<u>to</u> go, do <u>not</u> look].
Passive	a **clause** is **passive** where an (indirect) **object** is responsible for the action or feeling expressed within it [the ball is thrown <u>by the boy</u>].
Past	a form of the **verb** (or **participle**) or a **tense** used to express actions or feelings which occurred in the past.
Pejorative	**comparative** form expressing less than.
Perfect	an **aspect** indicating completed action; opposite of **imperfect**.
Person	a grammatical form of **pronoun** or **verb** used to refer to the speaker (first person), listener (second person) or another party (third person).
Personal	a **pronoun** used to show **person** [I, you, herself, them].
Pluperfect	an **aspect** indicating action completed prior to a time specified for implied; see **perfect**.
Plural	a word form expressing more than one or, sometimes, more than two [car<u>s</u>, child<u>ren</u>].
Possessive	a linguistic form (often a **case** or a **particle**) which expresses possession [<u>their</u>, <u>whose</u>, Rebecca<u>'s</u>].
Predicat(iv)e	a **clause** element giving information about the **subject**, typically including a **verb** and either an **object** or **adjective** [the boy <u>throws the ball</u>, the car <u>is blue</u>].
Prefix	a meaningful form inserted at the front of a word to alter its grammatical use [<u>a</u>wait, <u>un</u>usual].

Preposition	a word used in front of a **noun** (or its **adjectives**) which adds meaning or indicates grammatical role in the **clause**.
Present	a **tense** used to express actions or feelings which occur now.
Progressive	a **verb** form or phrase expressing continuation, duration or incompleteness [she is <u>going</u>].
Pronoun	a word which can substitute for a **noun** or **noun phrase** [she, which, it].
Reflexive	a construction where the subject and object refer to the same thing [<u>he</u> washed <u>himself</u>].
Relative	a **pronoun** used as a **subordinating conjunction** to refer back to the **noun** in the **main clause** (or to the main clause in its entirety).
Romance	used to refer to modern **Italic** languages.
Singular	a word form expressing one; in practice, opposite of **plural**.
Slavic	family of languages (including Russian, Polish and Serbian/Croatian), all deriving from a single common ancestor, which itself (like **Germanic** and **Latin**) derived from Proto-Indo-European.
Subject	a word (**noun/pronoun**) or group of words about which something is said in the clause [<u>the boy</u> throws the ball].
Subjunctive	a **verb** form (**mood**), used typically in **subordinate** clauses, to express uncertainty, wish or doubt; aligned to **conjunctive** in **Germanic**.
Subordinate	a **clause**, usually introduced by a **subordinating conjunction**, whose action or feeling is dependent on and provides further information about another clause [he came <u>because</u> she was there, they won <u>even though</u> they conceded first].
Subordinating	see **subordinate**.
Suffix	a meaningful form inserted at the end of a word to alter its meaning or grammatical use [do<u>es</u>, bigg<u>est</u>, play<u>er</u>].

Superlative	a form of **adjectives/adverbs** indicating positive overall comparison to other elements (usually **nouns/pronouns**) in the clause [big<u>gest</u>, <u>most</u> intelligent].
Syllable	a unit of pronunciation having one **vowel** sound.
Tense	a difference in **verb** form to show when the action, feeling or event took or takes place; tenses are generally considered to be **past** or **present** in **Germanic** languages, but **future** is added in **Latinate** languages and Esperanto, and **conditional** may also be considered.
Tonal	a language which distinguishes **vowels** by their tone, rather than (only) stress or quality.
Transitive	said of a **verb** taking an object [I spin the ball], as opposed to when it is used intransitively [I spin, I spin around] or a verb which cannot be used transitively [I fall].
Verb	a **part of speech** which expresses an action, feeling or event; may be marked for **person**, **tense, mood, aspect** or **voice** (either via endings or through added **auxiliary** verbs).
Verb phrase	a group of words which have the same function as a single **verb** [she <u>has been</u>, they <u>would see</u>].
Voice	defines the "doer" and "receiver" of the action expressed by the **verb** in a clause; in modern Western European languages **active** or **passive**.
Voicing	**consonants** are said to be voiced (*b, d, g, v, z* etc) or voiceless (*p, t, k, f, s* etc).
Vowel	a sound made without audible friction which can form the centre of a syllable (in English written <a>, <e>, <i>, <o>, <u> and occasionally <y>).
Word order	order in which words or **parts of speech** are placed in a **clause**.
Yes/no question	a question to which the answer is 'yes' or 'no' [Are you coming? Do you like apples?], also known as a "closed" or "polar" question.

A.2   Abbreviations and symbols

act.	active
fem.	feminine
imperf.	imperfect
masc.	masculine
perf.	perfect
PIE	Proto-Indo-European
pl.	plural
pluperf.	pluperfect
Port.	Portuguese
poss.	possessive
sg.	singular
SOV	subject, object, verb (word order)
subj.	subjunctive
SVO	subject, verb, object (word order)
VSO	verb, subject, object (word order)
V2	verb second element in clause

' '	used in this book to indicate English translations or words
" "	used in this book to mark names or citations
*	used to mark non-standard (or archaic) usage
[ ]	used to mark a written and approximate spoken form; or for additional clarification
< >	marks a written letter or letters
/ /	marks a spoken sound (using the International Phonetic Alphabet)

APPENDIX B

—

COMPARISON LISTS

B.1   Present forms of key verbs

'Be'		Latin	Italian	Spanish	Port.	French	German	Dutch
Sg.	1st	*sum*	*sono*	*soy*	*sou*	*suis*	*bin*	*ben*
	2nd	*es*	*sei*	*eres*	*és*	*es*	*bist*	*bent*
	3rd	*est*	*è*	*es*	*é*	*est*	*ist*	*is*
Pl.	1st	*sumus*	*siamo*	*somos*	*somos*	*sommes*	*sind*	*zijn*
	2nd	*estis*	*siete*	*sois*	*sois*	*êtes*	*seid*	*zijn*
	3rd	*sunt*	*sono*	*son*	*são*	*sont*	*sind*	*zijn*

Note:
- Danish *at være* – all persons singular and plural: *er*.
- Afrikaans *wees* – all persons singular and plural: *is*.

'Have'		Latin	Italian	Spanish	Port.	French	German	Dutch
Sg.	1st	*habeō*	*ho*	*he/tengo*	*tenho*	*ai*	*habe*	*heb*
	2nd	*habēs*	*hai*	*has/tienes*	*tens*	*as*	*hast*	*hebt*
	3rd	*habet*	*ha*	*ha/tiene*	*tem*	*a*	*hat*	*heeft*
Pl.	1st	*habēmus*	*abbiamo*	*hemos*	*temos*	*avons*	*haben*	*hebben*
	2nd	*habētis*	*avete*	*habeis*	*tendes*	*avez*	*habt*	*hebben*
	3rd	*habent*	*hanno*	*han*	*têm*	*ont*	*haben*	*hebben*

Note:
- Danish *at have* – all persons singular and plural: *har*.
- Afrikaans *hê* – all persons singular and plural: *het*.

Spanish has *haber* as auxiliary; *tener* as main verb (regular in plural).

B.2   Core vocabulary reference list

The range of meanings assigned to any given word will come to vary over time and will always differ somewhat from language to language (and even dialect to dialect). Therefore, vocabulary is best acquired through comprehensible input (17.2) and learned in context.

However, while noting that correspondences are rarely one to one (and even less so among commonly used words), a list of core vocabulary may be helpful for reference.

Latinate languages:

Latin	Italian	Spanish	French
circa	circa	más o menos	environ
dē	su	sobre	sur
post	dopo	después	depuis, après
rūrsus	ancora	otra vez	encore
tōtus, omnis	tutto, ogni	todo	tout
prope	quasi	casí	presque
iam	già	ya	déjà
etiam	anche	también	aussi
semper	sempre	siempre	toujours
et	e	y	et
malus	cattivo, malato	malo	mauvais
quia	perché	porque	parce que
ante	prima	antes	avant
magnus	grande	grande	grand
sed	ma, però	pero	mais
certus	certo	seguro	sûre
satis	abbastanza	bastante	assez
bonus	buono	bueno	bon
hīc	qui	aquí	ici
sī	se	si	si
sinister	sinistra	izquierda	gauche
minus	meno	menos	moins

COMPARISON LISTS

Latin	Italian	Spanish	French
plūs, magis	più	más	plus
necesse esse	avere bisogno	necesitar	avoir besoin de
novus	nuovo	nuevo	nouveau
nunc	ora, adesso	ahora	maintenant
vetus	vecchio	viejo	vieux
solum	solo	solo	seul
aut	o	o	ou
alius	altro	otro	autre
fortasse	forse	tal vez	peut-être
possibilis	possibile	posible	possible
satis	bastante	bastante	assez
vērē	veramente	realmente	vraiment
vērus	vero	verdad	vrai
dexter	destro	derecha	droite
īdem	stesso	mismo	même
parvus	piccolo	pequeño	petit
tam	così	tam	tellement
aliquis	alcuni	algunos	quelque
(ali)quis	qualcuno	alguién	quelqu'un
(ali)quis	qualcosa	algo	quelque chose
aliquandō	qualche volta	a veces	quelques fois
tamen	tuttavia	todavía	toujours
tālis	tale	tanto	tel
quam	come	que, como	que, comme
grātias	grazie	gracias	merci
quod	che	que	que
itaque	così	así	ainsi
illīc	là	allí	là
ergō	dunque	entonces	donc
rēs	cosa	cosa	chose
cāsus	volta	vez	fois
nimis	troppo	demasiado	trop
multum	molto	muy	très
falsus	falso	falso	faux
iuvenis	giovane	joven	jeune
paeniteō	scusa	disculpe	pardon
id est	è	es	c'est
esse	c'è, ci sono	hay	il y a

145

Germanic languages:

English	Danish	German	Dutch
about	omkring	etwa	ongeveer
about	om	über	over
after	efter	nach	achter
again	igen	wieder	nog
all	alle	alle	alle
almost	næsten	fast	bijna
already	allerede	schon	al
also	også	auch	ook
always	altid	immer	altijd
and	og	und	en
bad	dårlig	schlecht	slecht
because	fordi	weil	omdat
before	før	vor	voor
big	stor	groß	groot
but	men	aber	maar
certain	sikker	sicher	zeker
enough	nok	genug	genoeg
good	godt	gut	goet
here	her	hier	heer
if	hvis	wenn	als
left	venstre	links	links
less, fewer	mindre	weniger	minder
more	mere	mehr	meer
need	behøver	brauchen	nodig hebben
new	ny	neu	nieuw
now	nu	jetzt	nou
old	gammel	alt	oud
only	kun	nur	alleen
or	eller	oder	of
other	andre	anderer	ander
perhaps	måske	vielleicht	misschien
possible	mulig	möglich	mogelijk
quite	temmelig	ziemlich	heel
really	virkelig	wirklich	werkelijk
right	rigtig	richtig	waar

COMPARISON LISTS

English	Danish	German	Dutch
right	højre	rechts	rechts
same	samme	selber, gleicher	zelfde
small	lille	klein	kleen
so	så	so	zo
some	nogle	mancher	enige
someone	nogen	jemand	iemand
something	noget	etwas	iets
sometimes	nogle gange	manchmal	soms
still	stadigvæk	noch	nog
such	sådan nogle	solcher	zulk
than, as	end, som	als, wie	dan, als
thanks	tak	danke	bedankt
that	at	dass	dat
that way	sådan	so	zo
there	der	da	daar
therefore	derfor	deshalb	dus
thing	ting	Ding, Sache	ding
time	gang	Mal	keer
too	for	zu	te
very	meget	sehr	heel, zeer
wrong	forkert	falsch	verkeerd
young	ung	jung	jong
I'm sorry	undskyld	es tut mir leid	't spijt me
it's	det er	es ist	het is
there is/are	der er	es gibt	er is, er zijn

APPENDIX C

BIBLIOGRAPHY

C.1   Online resources

Gutman,   A.,   2014.   *The*   *Language*   *Gulper.* http://www.languagesgulper.com/eng/Home.html

Lynch, J., 2014. *Research Gate (Indo-European Language Tree).* https://www.researchgate.net/figure/Indo-European-language-tree-16_fig1_338989490

Oddone,   L.,   2020.   *Learn*   *Italian*   *with*   *Lucrezia.* https://learnitalianwithlucrezia.blog/

Rudder,   J.,   2013.   *Grammar*   *of*   *Romance.* http://nativlang.com/romance-languages

C.2   Further reading

Alkire, T. and Rosen, C., 2010. *Romance Languages – A Historical Introduction.* Cambridge: Cambridge University Press.

Beekes, R.S.P., 1995. *Comparative Indo-European Linguistics.* Leiden: John Benjamin.

Butt, J. and Benjamin, C., 2018. *A New Reference Grammar of Modern Spanish*. London: Routledge. (6th edition, reprint of 2018. First published by Arnold 1988)

Campbell, G.L., 1995. *Compendium of the World's Languages*. London: Routledge.

Durrell, M., 2011. *Hammer's German Grammar and Usage*. London: Hodder. (5th edition, reprint of 2011. First published by Arnold 1971)

Harrison, J.A., 1971. *Latin Reading Course*. London: Collins.

Hawkins, R. and Towell, R., 2015. *French Grammar and Usage*. London: Routledge. (4th edition, reprint of 2015. First published 1996)

Kalocsay, K. and Waringhein, G., 1985. *Plena Analiza Gramatiko de Esperanto*. Rotterdam: UEA. (5th edition, reprint of 1985. First published 1931)

Kaufmann, S., 2005. *The Way of the Linguist*. Vancouver: The Linguist.

Maiden, M. and Robustelli, C., 2007. *A Reference Grammar of Modern Italian*. London: Routledge. (2nd edition, reprint of 2007. First published by Hodder 2000)

Ørberg, H.H., 2011. *Familia Romana (Lingua Latina)*. Grenaa: Domus Latina.

Parsley, I.J., 2012. *Ulster Scots – A Short Reference Grammar*. Belfast: Ultonia.

Petrunin, M., 2018. *Comparative Grammar of Spanish, Portuguese, Italian and French*. Seattle: Amazon.

Ranieri, L.A., 2017. *Ranieri Reverse Recall*. Philadelphia: Aquellia.

Printed in Great Britain
by Amazon

85278052R00092